D1626216

The Arctic Fox

The Arctic Fox

Francis Leopold McClintock
Discoverer of the fate of Franklin

David Murphy

The Collins Press

Printed in Ireland in 2004 by
The Collins Press
West Link Park
Doughcloyne,
Wilton,
Cork

Published in North America by
Dundern Press, 8 Market Street
Suite 200, Toronto ON, M5E 1M6
ISBN 1-55002-523-6

British Library Cataloguing in Publication Data
Murphy, David
The Arctic fox : Francis Leopold McClintock, discoverer of the fate
of Franklin
1. M'Clintock, Sir Francis Leopold, 1819–1907
2. Great Britain. Royal Navy – Biography
3. Explorers – Ireland – Biography
4. Northwest Passage – Discovery and exploration – British
I. Title
917.1'95041

ISBN 1 903464 58 7

Typesetting: Dominic Carroll, Co. Cork
Cover design: Artmark, Cork
Printing: Creative Print and Design (Wales) Ltd, Ebbw Vale

For James McGuire

CONTENTS

LIST OF ILLUSTRATIONS

A NOTE ON TERMINOLOGY

During the period covered in this book, the word Eskimo (or Esquimaux) was in common use. Of the word Eskimo, the *Oxford English Dictionary* has this to say:

> Some people believe that it is better to use the term Inuit rather than Eskimo, because they think that Eskimo could be seen as offensive. The term Eskimo, however, is the only term that correctly covers both the Inuit (people of northern Canada, and parts of Greenland and Alaska) and the Yupik (people of Siberia, the Aleutian Islands and Alaska), and is still widely used.
>
> *Oxford English Dictionary* (Oxford, 2002)

Given that this book refers only to the inhabitants of Greenland, northern Canada and Alaska, the term Inuit is used in preference to Eskimo in the main body of the text, while the term Eskimo is used only in quoted text.

ACKNOWLEDGEMENTS

A significant number of people gave me advice, encouragement and practical help while writing this book, and they are all deserving of my thanks.

I would like to thank everyone at the Scott Polar Research Institute (SPRI) in Cambridge, many of whom went out of their way to help me during my research visits. Deserving of special mention is Robert Headland, who was always available with his vast knowledge, keen insight and infectious enthusiasm. I would like to thank Caroline Gunn for her help and also for deciphering McClintock's dreadful handwriting on a couple of occasions. I am very grateful to Lucy Martin of SPRI's photographic archive for organising some of the illustrations for this book. It was with extreme regret that I learned early in 2004 of the death of William Mills, librarian and keeper of collections at SPRI. William was always friendly and helpful to those who sought his advice, and I am just one of the many researchers who were assisted by his encyclopaedic knowledge of polar exploration.

I am indebted to the staff of the Royal Irish Academy library who provided both practical assistance and a place of scholarly escape. My special thanks go to Siobhán Fitzpatrick, Petra Schnabel, Dymphna Moore, Patrick Kelly and Karl Vogelsang. The staff of the Early Printed Books Library in Trinity College, Dublin gave me invaluable help yet again, and my thanks go to Charles Benson, Shane Mawe and Rose Reddy.

Since 1997 I have worked with the Royal Irish Academy's *Dictionary of Irish Biography*, and it was through this project that I first became interested in Irish polar explorers in general and McClintock in particular. I owe my colleagues at the *Dictionary of Irish Biography* a particular debt of gratitude, and wish to thank James Quinn, Richard Hawkins, C.J. Woods, Helen Andrews and Linde Lunny.

The National Museum of Ireland was also forthcoming with much assistance, and I would like to thank Eamon Kelly (keeper of antiquities), Rachel Hand (ethnographical officer) and Josephine McGlade of the museum's photographic department.

Nigel Monaghan of the Natural History Museum in Merrion Square was also particularly helpful, and I am grateful for being allowed to reproduce photographs of some of the zoological specimens in the museum's collection.

In similar vein, the assistance of Helen Trompeteler at the National Portrait Gallery in London was most helpful, and I am grateful for permission to reproduce images of portraits of McClintock in the gallery's collection.

I am particularly grateful to Frank Nugent, mountaineer, explorer and writer. Despite the fact that Frank was busy writing his own book on Irish polar explorers – *Seek the Frozen Lands* – he was generous with both his time and research, while also providing his own unique insight into the exploits of these Victorian explorers. I also wish to thank Jonathan Shackleton for the advice he gave me during the early phase of this research.

A strong Canadian theme ran through my researches, and my gratitude goes to several people in that vast country. I particularly wish to thank William Barr, previously of the University of Calgary; it was a great honour to get useful advice from such a prolific writer of polar history. I also wish to thank Frank Duerden of Ryerson University, and Stephen Reynolds, organiser of the Canadian side of the Yukon Quest sled-dog race. My thanks also go to Anne and Frank Turner of Mutuk Kennels, Whitehorse, Yukon Territory.

During the course of my research, I victimised many of my friends by keeping them up to date with this book's progress. Many of them gave their time to discuss the project, and for this I will always be grateful. My thanks go to Tony Gaynor, Adam Pole, Anthony McCormack, Ciaran Diamond, Barbara Lendaro, Phil Lecane, Tom Burke, Fergus O'Donoghue and Todd Morrissey. I am also grateful for the patience and support of my parents and sister. By this stage, all of the above know more about polar exploration than they ever needed to.

My special thanks go to Dominic Carroll.

For over a decade now, I have known James McGuire of University College, Dublin and the *Dictionary of Irish Biography*. I initially met James when he supervised my MA, and since that time he has shown himself to be a true friend and mentor. I am sure there are many young scholars who would say similar things about James. He gave me my first chance to work as an historian, and for that I will always be grateful. This book is dedicated to him.

Sir Francis Leopold McClintock.

A Victorian Icon

This expedition has been the favourite dream
of my early years. I have read with ardour the
accounts of the various voyages which have
been made in the prospect of arriving at the
North Pacific Ocean through the seas which
surround the pole. You may remember that a
history of all the voyages made for purposes of
discovery composed the whole of our good
uncle Thomas's library. My education was
neglected, yet I was passionately fond of
reading. These volumes were my study, day and
night.

Walton's first letter in
Mary Shelley's *Frankenstein*.[1]

The last decade has seen a resurgent interest in polar
exploration, focused largely on the great Edwardian
explorers – men such as Captain Robert Scott, Sir Ernest
Shackleton, Captain Lawrence 'Titus' Oates, Dr Edward
Wilson, Apsley Cherry-Garrard and Tom Crean. Anyone
familiar with the history of polar exploration will recognise
these names and know that these men were all Antarctic

explorers. Such men were, however, the adventurous descendants of an earlier generation of polar explorers who, for the most part, were engaged in Arctic exploration.

The nineteenth century had been an era of great explorers, most famous among them being David Livingstone and Sir Henry Morton Stanley – renowned for their African explorations – and Sir Richard Francis Burton and John Hanning Speke, who for years searched for the source of the Nile. Hardly a year passed in which the national newspapers or the journals of learned societies were not crammed with reports of various expeditions. The public became gripped by 'expedition mania', avidly collecting accounts of these voyages and flocking to town halls and lecture venues, such as the Royal Geographical Society, to listen to reports of the latest expedition to the Congo or to the Arabian deserts.

The excitement surrounding exploration inspired the most unlikely of characters to head off on expeditions of their own. Perhaps the most notable example of this phenomenon occurred in 1848 when Lady Margaret Harriet Kavanagh (1800–85), an Irish widow of considerable means, undertook an expedition with her young children. Having toured Turkey, Egypt and the Holy Land, she completed a crossing of the Sinai Desert, reaching Aqaba in 36 days; this at a time when European travellers were uncommon in the region and when the idea of a European woman crossing Sinai would have been considered preposterous.[2]

While nineteenth-century expeditions sought to solve various geographical problems, one region in particular attracted most attention. During the course of the century numerous expeditions were dispatched to the Arctic with a single goal – to discover the Northwest Passage. The search for this Arctic sea route became a

Victorian obsession, with expeditions being undertaken at great cost in both financial and human terms. Some of the most prominent figures in these expeditions were Irish, among them Captain F.R.M. Crozier, Captain Henry Kellett and Captain Robert McClure. One among them, however, was to achieve fame far surpassing that of his fellow Irish explorers: that man was Sir Francis Leopold McClintock. Between 1848 and 1859 McClintock took part in just four Arctic expeditions yet managed to carve out a significant niche for himself in the history of Arctic exploration. All his expeditions were in search of Sir John Franklin, who had disappeared in the Arctic in 1845 with two ships and more than 120 men while searching for the Northwest Passage. During McClintock's last expedition – the *Fox* expedition of 1857–59 – he found debris from the Franklin expedition scattered along the coast of King William Island, while one of McClintock's officers – Lieutenant William R. Hobson – discovered a vital document left behind by Franklin's men. It provided an outline of their fate, and remains the only document to be recovered from the expedition.

It was the findings of the *Fox* expedition that secured McClintock his place in the pantheon of polar explorers. Less celebrated has been his innovations in the areas of sledge travel, Arctic equipment and cooking methods. During his expeditions to trace Franklin, McClintock pioneered the use of storage depots and satellite parties to lengthen the distance a sledge expedition could cover. Still remembered by a few as the father of modern sledge travel, some of his methods continue to be employed today. McClintock also possessed immense scientific curiosity, and brought back fossils, zoological specimens and ethnographical material – items later donated to collections in Ireland, Britain and Denmark.

Despite having been a Victorian icon, McClintock is now virtually forgotten. Aside from a handful of polar-history enthusiasts, very few will have heard the name of Sir Francis Leopold McClintock. Yet he was the Ernest Shackleton of his day – a leader, a motivator and, above all, a survivor.

Today, the idea of getting excited about the activities of a polar explorer might seem quaint. Modern surveying technology ensures that the world can now be mapped by satellites, and there are really no areas which remain unknown to geographical science. Equally, satellite communications and GPS systems ensure the safety of modern explorers. But in McClintock's day the maps and charts of the world were covered with unknown areas, and the men who ventured out to explore these regions did so in the knowledge that, should things go wrong, there would be little chance of rescue. They were the astronauts of their day, and this fact must be grasped if one is to understand the fascination in which they were held. To the nineteenth-century public, both in Ireland and across the world, McClintock was one of the most fascinating of all.

This book aims, then, to provide a sketch of his life while outlining his importance as a polar explorer. Where appropriate, McClintock's own words have been repro-duced to give the reader an impression of the character of the man. Hopefully, it will illustrate just why he achieved such renown in his own lifetime.

CHAPTER ONE

A Brief Irish Childhood

Francis Leopold McClintock was born into a family with a long and interesting history in Ireland. The McClintocks were descended from Alexander McClintock from Argyllshire, who had moved to Ireland in the seventeenth century, buying the estate at Trintagh, County Donegal in 1597. A tough Scot, he was one of the many planters who consolidated British rule in Ireland during this period and, over the course of the next few centuries, the McClintock family prospered. Indeed, by the middle of the twentieth century, there were offshoots of the family living in Counties Antrim, Armagh, Carlow, Donegal, Louth, Tyrone and Tipperary, with numerous members of the family having become quite wealthy and prominent in the political life of the country. Among them was Francis Leopold McClintock's grandfather, John McClintock (1742–99), who owned a large estate at Drumcar, County Louth and who was successively Member of Parliament for Enniskillen (1783–90) and Belturbet (1790–97).[3]

The McClintock men tended to have large families – John McClintock fathered four sons, the last of whom was Henry McClintock, Francis Leopold McClintock's father. In keeping with inheritance practice of the time, the eldest son was left the family estate while the younger sons struggled to make a career in the Church, the army or the navy. Henry McClintock, born in 1783, was no exception. He joined the army and was commissioned into the 3rd Dragoons, while his eldest brother, John (1769–1855), inherited the family estate at Drumcar, became chief sergeant-at-arms for Ireland and later Member of Parliament for Athlone (1823) and County Louth (1831). While his eldest brother enjoyed a successful political career, Henry would seem to have been dissatisfied with his career in the army. In 1809 he resigned his commission, and was appointed as collector of customs at Dundalk in County Louth, a modest enough position for a young man from so influential a family. In December 1809 he married Elizabeth Melesina Fleury, daughter of the Venerable George Fleury, archdeacon of Waterford. They followed the McClintock tradition of raising very large families and together had no less than fourteen children, two of whom died in infancy, including Louis, their eldest son.[4]

Francis Leopold McClintock was born on 8 July 1819, the second but ultimately eldest surviving son. Although christened Francis Leopold, he was usually referred to as 'Leopold', and even in later life preferred to use the form 'Sir F. Leopold McClintock' (his preferred Leopold is used in this volume). At the time of his birth, the family was living at 1 Seatown Place, Dundalk, a rather ordinary looking three-storey town house. The house still stands, bearing a small plaque indicating that one of the greatest-ever polar explorers once lived there. Educated at the local grammar school – run by the Reverend John Darley (later the bishop of Meath) – Leopold enjoyed a happy and active childhood. His parents seem to have loved their numerous children, and his childhood passed in outdoor

*1 Seatown Place, Dundalk: the birthplace of McClintock. The house
now bears a plaque indicating that McClintock once lived there.*

pursuits, his father taking him shooting and fishing along the banks of the Rivers Dee and Fane in County Louth. Leopold and his siblings were taken on expeditions to the Cooley and Mourne mountains, and to see local field antiquities, most notably the massive Proleek dolman.

It soon became apparent that the young Leopold was more suited to an active and outdoor lifestyle. He found the lessons at the Reverend Darley's school ponderous in the extreme, and especially hated his classical and Latin studies. A Church career was closed to him as a result of this inattention, and it became increasingly likely that he would follow a career in the army or navy. He later recalled that, as a boy, he had been greatly impressed by a portrait of Admiral Berkeley that hung in his father's room, and liked to imagine what the life of a sailor would be like.

Leopold's cousin, William Bunbury McClintock, was then a lieutenant in the Royal Navy and, benefiting from useful contacts, was given the disposal of the position of first-class volunteer aboard HMS *Samarang*. In a letter dated 20 June 1831 he wrote to Leopold's father, offering the position to his son. Leopold's clothes and belongings were quickly packed and, on the very afternoon the letter was received, young Leopold took the mail coach to Dublin. From Dublin, he travelled by mail boat to Bristol and then took another coach to Portsmouth. On 22 June 1831 he was officially appointed as a first-class volunteer aboard the *Samarang*.[5] It was the beginning of a naval career that would span more than 50 years, yet he was not yet twelve years old.

The idea of sending such a young child to sea seems both incredible and cruel by today's standards, but almost two centuries ago was considered quite acceptable. The Royal Navy at that time was organised along Nelsonian lines, and was renowned for its harsh discipline, poor pay, sub-standard food and cramped living conditions. During long sea voyages, ships' crews braved the fiercest storms, while shipboard diseases, foremost among them scurvy, were common. In short, naval life of the period was monotonous, uncomfortable and often downright danger-ous. The routine of shipboard life could instil a mind-numbing boredom, while a moment's inattention aloft in the yards could result in a fatal fall to the deck.

Leopold's position as first-class volunteer was a lowly one indeed – in fact, the lowest rung on the career ladder for potential officers. These positions were usually in the gift of a captain, who would pick members of his family – or the sons of friends – to fill vacancies. When the requi-site amount of 'sea-time' had been built up, the young volunteer could apply to sit the examination for promo-tion to midshipman. The next step up the promotion ladder would be to pass as a ship's mate (sub-lieutenant), and then as a lieutenant. The practice of patronage was, of course, open to abuse, and it was not uncommon for a captain to falsely enter in his log the names of family members, and in this way create for them fictitious records of sea-time. The young McClintock found himself well placed in terms of patronage, with his cousin, William Bunbury McClintock, as first lieutenant aboard the *Sama-rang*, while its captain, Charles H. Paget – son of Admiral the Honourable Sir Charles Paget – treated Leopold as a favourite, and saw to it that he received extra food. Paget would later marry McClintock's sister, Emily Caroline. For the first years of his naval career, then, Leopold enjoyed the patronage of these useful connections.

When he joined the ship, McClintock was only 4 feet 6 inches tall and weighed 68 pounds, just 2 pounds more than the first lieutenant's Newfoundland dog. In a rather pathetic letter home, he remarked, 'I like everyone in the ship, particularly Captain Paget's little lovely lap-dog'. Nicknamed 'Pat' or 'Paddy' by the crew, Leopold was still very much a child and given only light duties.

The *Samarang* left Plymouth in July 1831 and would not return to a British port for more than three years, providing ample time for McClintock to learn his profession of seaman. The days were not entirely dull, and Leopold engaged in his share of skylarking, having at least one fall from the yards due to a lapse of attention – he fell over 60 feet but landed on coils of rope, and was fortunate not to be seriously injured.

The *Samarang* – 113 feet long and a mere 500 tons – called to the Azores en route to its South American station. As the ship cruised off the coast of Brazil and called to the Gulf of California, McClintock was appointed boat midshipman. In late 1834 the *Samarang* was based at Callao in Brazil when one of the ship's officers, Lieutenant W. Smyth, was given permission to undertake an expedition across the Andes and from there descend the Amazon. Accompanied by Midshipman Frederick Lowe, Smyth prepared for the journey, affording the young McClintock his first insight into how such an expedition should be planned. Smyth and Lowe ultimately descended the Amazon, being only the second English expedition to do so. Smyth would carry out further voyages of exploration and, some years later, would be instrumental in setting McClintock on the path to polar explorer.

The *Samarang* returned to Portsmouth in January 1835, and McClintock was granted a period of leave. He spent four months at the family home in Dundalk before joining his next ship, the *Carron* – a survey ship engaged in mapping around the Isle of Man. His new captain was most unpleasant and Leopold did not enjoy this commission.

As the ship's only midshipman, he worked long, hard hours, and was glad when the cruise ended at Woolwich in November 1835.

A further period of leave followed, which he spent fishing in the River Fane and shooting in the fields around Dundalk. On one occasion he was careless with his gun and caused it to go off while resting on the ground, badly scorching his cheek and affecting the sight in his right eye. He feared that he might lose the eye altogether, but after a few days, his sight fortunately recovered.

There were indications that his time at sea had made him much more adventurous. As a variation on his shipboard skylarking, he climbed to the roof of the church in Dundalk in order to explore it.

His next ship was the *Crocodile*, which he joined in Bermuda in April 1838. The vessel was initially commanded by Captain Polkinhorne, but upon Polkinhorne's death in 1839 Captain Alexander Milne took command. This period in the *Crocodile* was an important one for McClintock, during which he passed his seamanship exam – on 23 October 1838 – and was made acting-mate, the equivalent of a modern-day sub-lieutenant. Based in the West Indies, the *Crocodile* was engaged in the anti-slavery campaign, and McClintock was involved in the capture of the slave-ship *Mercedita*. He was one of the prize crew that took the ship to Havana and he later received £7 in prize money.

This period in the *Crocodile* brought him up and down the coast of the Americas, enabling him to visit Bolivia and serve off the coast of Newfoundland. When he was due to sit the examination for lieutenant – which would hopefully bring further promotion – McClintock travelled to Plymouth aboard the *Ringdove*, arriving there on 25 September 1841. The next year or more would be spent aboard the *Excellent*, where he was trained as a gunnery officer, and also at the Royal Naval College, where he took classes in engineering, navigation and seamanship. He was successful in his gunnery course, and obtained a first-class certificate in steam machinery and a second-class certificate in mathematics. But in the hard-fought competition for a first-lieutenant's commission, McClintock was unsuccessful. He had chosen to study steam machinery since it was obvious to all young officers that the Royal Navy would eventually become a steam-powered navy. Since his early teens – one could even say his childhood – he had been trained to be a leader of men and was now qualified as a surveyor, navigator and gunnery officer. Yet a first lieutenant's commission still eluded him, and this would cast a shadow over the next phase of his career.

In January 1843 he was appointed gunnery officer aboard the *Gorgon*, which was earmarked for the Brazilian station. McClintock joined his new ship as a young officer who no longer enjoyed the benefits of patronage, and this next commission would prove crucial in his career. If he did not impress his new commander, Captain Charles Hotham, he might be unable to progress and could easily end up as one of those ship's mates imprisoned in the lower echelons of the service, with no hope of further promotion.

Wrestling the Gorgon

M cClintock's time as a mate aboard the *Gorgon* was to mark an important and hectic phase in his career. The *Gorgon*, which weighed 1,142 tons, was one of the Royal Navy's new paddle steamers, and was sent to the South Atlantic to join the Brazilian squadron. This was a particularly volatile time in South America as, in October 1838, a revolution had broken out in Uruguay. Two rival groups – the Colorados, who represented the landed gentry, and the Blancos, who claimed to represent the common man – were battling to control the country. Montevideo was besieged by the Colorado army led by General Don Manuel Oribe. In June 1843 the *Gorgon* arrived off Montevideo to join a Royal Navy squadron sent to protect British trading interests in the area and, if necessary, to evacuate British subjects.

Between June 1843 and May 1844 McClintock and his shipmates cruised up and down off Montevideo. It was a most unusual situation and, while Britain was not technically at war, a state of full alert had to be maintained in case of further outbreaks of violence ashore. For McClintock, it was an especially difficult time. He was still only a ship's mate and, without powerful patrons, knew he could only gain further promotion by distinguishing himself in some way. Having reached his mid-twenties, some advance in his career had to come soon. Yet ploughing up and down off Montevideo provided him with little opportunity to distinguish himself. Then – as he bordered on despair – just such an opportunity presented itself. Ironically, it was preceded by an event that could have killed both McClintock and the entire crew of the *Gorgon*.

On 10 May 1844 a violent storm developed off Montevideo and, as the ferocity of the gale increased, the *Gorgon* – which was lying at an outer mooring – began to drag its anchors. The engineers got up steam and Captain Hotham tried to make for open water, but the storm was too violent. In the midst of mountainous seas and howling winds, the *Gorgon* was driven inshore and it became increasingly obvious that they were about to run aground; it would later be learnt that nine other merchant ships were driven ashore and completely wrecked during the storm. Fortunately, the *Gorgon* came to rest above the tide line, embedded in the wide and sandy beach off Montevideo. To the great relief of McClintock and the crew, the vessel settled down – still intact – in over 13 feet of sand. Yet while all aboard were safe, the next morning revealed just how deeply the *Gorgon* was embedded. Totally beached and over 1,000 yards from open water, refloating the ship seemed to be an impossibility. But Captain Hotham refused to abandon his ship, and this decision was ultimately to offer McClintock the chance he so desperately sought to prove himself.

The first attempts to refloat the *Gorgon* followed what were perhaps predictable lines. The ship was lightened, all excess equipment, food and coal being taken off. Then, cables were run to points on other ships and ashore. Using its own engine for motive power, the *Gorgon* tried to pull itself free from the clinging sand, budging not an inch. While another commander might have despaired, Captain Hotham was determined to save his ship, and now announced the final and somewhat extreme option: the crew of the *Gorgon* would dig the ship free.

During the next five months the officers and men laboured night and day on what must have seemed an impossible task. The idea of freeing a beached ship purely through manual labour is astonishing, but this is what McClintock and his shipmates did, and McClintock's value was seen and recognised in the endeavour. Firstly, the ship's masts and rigging were stripped away, and all equipment – including the ship's guns – was moved ashore. Next, the sand was dug out from around the ship – a monumental task that did not cease until more than 19,000 tons of sand had been excavated from beneath the *Gorgon*'s hull.

A dock area was constructed alongside the ship, and when the *Gorgon*'s hull had been freed from the sand, piles were driven into the sand, and the banks created by the excavations reinforced with mortar. The removal of the sand created another problem, whereby the *Gorgon* – standing free of the sand – had to be shored up. When the ship finally stood free, the crew faced up to one more grim reality – the vessel still lay over 1,000 yards from open water. Applying themselves to yet another desperately laborious task, the men dredged a channel through the mud. Finally, empty casks were secured to the hull to act as buoyancy aides, while steam jacks were connected fore and aft to help lighten the load and lift the *Gorgon* through the channel. Cables had been run out to other ships – the *Alfred* and the *Philomel* – and all was now ready for the attempt to drag the ship to open sea.

On 26 September 1844 the steam jacks raised the ship while pressure was put on the cables. The *Gorgon* moved a mere 13 feet – no doubt terribly frustrating for McClintock and his shipmates. Another attempt was made on 13 October, and this time the ship moved 320 yards towards open water. By 19 October it had moved another 800 yards and, on 1 November, the *Gorgon* was once again afloat, almost six months after it had been driven ashore. This incredible feat would later be recorded in a book, *The Recovery of HMS* Gorgon, by Astley Cooper Key.[6]

McClintock had been prominent in the efforts to free the ship, labouring ceaselessly on the excavation works. He had gained important experience, much of which would later be of use to him in the Arctic. His efforts were not to go unrewarded. Captain Hotham heaped praise on all his men, reserving particular credit for McClintock. In a letter to McClintock's mother, prior to the ship being refloated, Hotham had written:

> The ship your son is serving in now lies aground in a situation which renders her removal difficult beyond measure. It is on these occasions that a captain forms his opinion as to the abilities and merits of his several officers; and I can confidently assure you that none stand higher in my estimation than your son. He is, without exception, one of the steadiest, most zealous and excellent young men that I have ever served with, and is deserving of his promotion or any other favour the Admiralty might confer upon him.[7]

This was not just empty praise. The commander of the Brazilian squadron, Commodore Purvis, informed Captain

Hotham that he could reward one of his junior officers with a lieutenant's commission, telling him he should choose the man who had most distinguished himself in the *Gorgon* affair. Without hesitation, Hotham chose McClintock. At last, he had received a lieutenant's commission, and his future looked more hopeful.

McClintock's next posting was aboard the *Frolic*, on the Pacific station, where he took part in the guarding of convoys of silver. In 1847 the crew of the *Frolic* was engaged in salvaging an English merchant ship in Punta Arenas. The ship had been sunk in the harbour while carrying over £8,000 in silver, and McClintock and his shipmates landed the vessel on the beach and recovered the cargo. In many ways, it was the *Gorgon* operation in reverse, and he was ideally suited to carry out such salvage work.

Returning to England in June 1847 the crew of the *Frolic* was paid off. McClintock continued on to Dublin for some well-earned leave, and stayed with his mother at 2 Gardiner Place, where she had lived since the death of her husband in February 1843. Though happy to be on leave, McClintock was no doubt keen to learn of his next commission; while he had carried out some unusual duties aboard the *Gorgon* and the *Frolic*, he must have assumed that he would now return to regular naval duty. But his next posting would completely alter the direction of his life, and mark the beginning of his career as a polar explorer. His first excursion to the Arctic, however, would not be a straightforward mission of exploration; rather, McClintock was to take part in a voyage to discover the fate of one of the most famous explorers in the world, Sir John Franklin.

Sir John Franklin, c. 1820.

CHAPTER THREE

The Unfortunate Franklin

During the course of his career as a polar explorer, Leopold McClintock would travel on four major expeditions, all of them in search of Sir John Franklin's missing Northwest Passage expedition. Franklin was one of the most high-profile polar explorers of the period, an all-round naval hero who had become a well-known public figure. In 1845 the Admiralty had sent him on expedition to the Arctic to discover the Northwest Passage. Never to return, Franklin's fate would later be discovered by Leopold McClintock.

The history of the search for the Northwest Passage is a long one. From Elizabethan times, a succession of sailors tried to find a route to the Pacific through the Arctic. Generations of geographers, sailors and explorers believed that such a route existed, and that ships intending to reach the Pacific could head northwest and negotiate their way through the islands of the Canadian Arctic archipelago, eventually emerging into the Pacific through the Bering Strait. One must remember that the search for this route predated the construction of both the Panama and Suez canals; during the greater part of the nineteenth century, there were no man-made shortcuts to enable ships reach the Pacific and Indian Oceans, and a voyage from a European port to the Pacific necessitated a long and dangerous voyage entailing negotiation of the Cape of Good Hope or, worse still, the treacherous Cape Horn. Odd as it may seem today, the idea of a route through the Arctic ice was immensely appealing.[8]

An early trailblazer was Martin Frobisher, who explored the area during the years 1576–78. Less than a decade later – in 1585 – a contemporary of Frobisher, John Davis, embarked on the first of his three voyages in search of the Northwest Passage, and was to venture into the Arctic Circle twice more in 1586–87. Successive generations of explorers – among them Henry Hudson and William Baffin – searched the eastern coasts of America, and ventured into the Arctic in search of a passage that would cut months off a voyage to the Pacific.

The search was renewed in the early nineteenth century due to the influence of John Barrow (1764–1848), a man appointed second secretary to the Admiralty in 1804 during the hectic period of the Napoleonic Wars. As well as being a capable Admiralty official during the war, he was a man of vast geographical curiosity and ambition, and was determined to fill in some of the 'blank spaces' on the Admiralty charts. Following the final defeat of Napoleon at Waterloo in 1815 Barrow found himself in partial charge of a vast navy that had been built up to counter the Napoleonic threat. Realising that these ships and men must be put to some use if the Royal Navy was not to be vastly reduced in size, he determined to utilise these resources to solve a series of geographical problems that had been troubling him for many years.[9]

Barrow's first attempt at organising an expedition ended in disaster. In 1816 he dispatched the Cork-born James Hingston Tuckey to West Africa to explore the

Congo. Tuckey was an experienced sailor and surveyor, but soon after arriving in the Congo his crew began to fall ill with yellow fever. Tuckey managed to navigate 200 miles upriver and explore further inland on foot before he himself succumbed to yellow fever and perished, along with a majority of his crew.[10]

John Barrow was undaunted, and later in his career sent further expeditions to Africa. In 1818, however, he turned to the Arctic, and dispatched an expedition in search of the Northwest Passage. Captain John Ross, Lieutenant Edward Parry, Captain David Buchan and Lieutenant John Franklin sailed the ships *Isabella*, *Alexander*, *Trent* and *Dorothea* to the Arctic, thus marking the beginning of a series of such expeditions. The search for the Northwest Passage developed into an obsession with Barrow, his reasons many and varied: the discovery of a passage would be beneficial to commerce as it was thought it would cut down the length of voyages to India; its discovery would enhance the prestige of British sailors in the eyes of the public; and it was a matter of national pride to outdo the French and Russians in geographical discoveries.

The fear of Russian expansionism was to increase during Barrow's term of office, and would greatly influence later attempts to find a Northwest Passage. In 1828 an obscure Irish army officer, Colonel Sir George De Lacy Evans (1787–1870), published *On the Designs of Russia* in which he predicted that the Russian army would eventually move southwards through Afghanistan to threaten Britain's possessions in India. The concerns prompted by the publication generated what came to be known as 'Russophobia', and for the remainder of the century, Russia was considered the great enemy, waiting to swallow up British India. This paranoia resulted in the long-term espionage war in Afghanistan and India – the 'Great Game' – and there existed a tremendous fear of conflict with Russia, a conflict that did eventually materialise in the shape of the Crimean War of 1854–56.

'Russophobia' gave the quest to find the Northwest Passage added impetus. Not only might Britain beat Russia in finding this route, its discovery would give the Royal Navy a strategic advantage: the ability to speedily send its warships to attack the Russian fleet in the Pacific. The various expeditions sent in search of a Northwest Passage, then, were motivated by both commerce and matters of state. But some of the advantages it was claimed would accrue from the discovery were quickly proven to be unfounded. For instance, if the passage was to be of any strategic or commercial value, it would obviously have to be a quick and easy route. The first expeditions, however, brought back ample evidence that the Northwest Passage would be nothing of the sort.

In light of discoveries made by Peter Dease and Thomas Simpson during their 1836–39 overland expedition to the Canadian Arctic, Barrow felt that the final discovery of the passage was close, and persuaded the Admiralty to send an expedition. Several possible leaders were considered, but after constant lobbying by his friends, the Admiralty gave Franklin the command, despite his being 59 years old. The noted explorer, Sir Edward Parry, commented to Lord Haddington, the first lord of the Admiralty, 'If you don't let him go, the man will die of disappointment'.

In March 1845 Franklin took command of HMS *Erebus*. A born sailor, the details of Franklin's career could well have been lifted from the pages of a C.S. Forester or Patrick O'Brian seafaring novel. Born at Spilsby in Lincolnshire in 1786, he was the youngest son in a family of twelve children. Like McClintock, Franklin had entered the Royal Navy as a boy sailor, joining in 1800 at the age of fourteen. He began his career on a survey mission to Australia, and was wrecked off the Cato Bank. In 1804 he was a member of the squadron that defeated the French Admiral Linois, and then served as signal midshipman aboard the *Bellorophon* during the Battle of Trafalgar. Promoted to lieutenant in 1808, he served on the American station and took part in the expedition against New Orleans during the American-British War (1812–14).

Franklin's career as a polar explorer commenced in 1818 when he was given command of the *Trent* and directed to accompany Captain David Buchan of the *Dorothea* in an attempt to reach the North Pole. Leaving England in April 1818 they travelled west of Spitzbergen until they were stopped by pack ice. On 30 July the ships were driven into the pack and were forced to shelter in Magdelena Bay. The *Dorothea* was badly damaged, and Buchan and Franklin decided to turn for home, arriving in England on 22 October 1818. It was an inauspicious beginning to an explorer's career that would eventually gain worldwide attention.

In 1819 Franklin was appointed to command a land expedition to the northern coast of the American continent – modern-day Canada – and carry out a survey of the Arctic coast. The North West Company and the Hudson's Bay Company undertook to supply the expedition. Landing at Fort York on the western side of Hudson Bay on 30 August 1819, Franklin intended to travel northwards with his party, assisted by a group of native Americans who would supply them with food. The small party of 23 men carried portable canoes with which they planned to cross the various lakes and rivers that crossed their route to the north, among them the Nelson, Elk and Coppermine Rivers and the Great Slave Lake. They

Lieut. Couch

Lieut. Fairholme

C.H. Osmer

Lieut. Des Vœux

Captain Crozier, *Terror*

Captain Sir John Franklin

Commander Fitzjames, *Erebus*

Lieut. Graham Gore (Commander)

Stanley (surgeon)

Lieut. H.T.D. Le Vesconte

Lieut. R.O. Sargent

James Read

J.H. Goodsir (asst. surgeon)

H.F. Collins

Portraits of Sir John Franklin and members of crew.

also took with them a considerable amount of unnecessary scientific equipment and even reference books.

The whole affair was a disaster from the very beginning. It was a poor year for wild game, and the native American hunting party supplied virtually no fresh meat, while the two trading companies, engaged in an unofficial war with one other, provided little or no supplies. When Franklin left Fort Chipewyan on 18 July 1820 his party carried just one day's provisions and a small supply of gunpowder. Nevertheless, he led his men northwards and, crossing the Great Slave Lake, they spent the winter of 1820–21 in a hut at the mouth of the Coppermine River. In June 1821 they set out in their boats to survey the north-eastern coastline, naming Cape Barrow and Cape Flinders. By mid-August, however, Franklin realised that their provisions would not hold out and they headed for home, turning back at a point that was aptly christened Cape Turnagain.

Though the survey mission had been a moderate success, the return journey to Fort Providence was to be a living nightmare. Retreating southwards in the face of the deepening winter, food became increasingly scarce, there being virtually no game available for the hunting parties. Rivers were only crossed with extreme difficulty, and as they travelled through the 'Barren Lands' of Canada, they continually discarded excess equipment in the hope of reaching Fort Providence. Franklin's party, slowly disintegrating, was forced to feed off deer carcasses, and even the smallest animals caught on hunting forays were seen as a huge boon, while a meal of mice became a delicacy. They also ate rock lichen – ironically dubbed 'tripes de roche' – and stewed their spare boots and shoes to provide desperately needed meals.

Members of the party fell down dead on the trial or

simply fell behind and were never seen again. Numbed with cold and racked by starvation, Franklin's men – becoming increasingly desperate – broke into smaller groups. One of these groups consisted of Surgeon (later Sir) John Richardson, Midshipman Thomas Hood, Seaman John Hepburn, a small number of Canadian voyageurs and an Iroquois by the name of Michel Ferohaite (sometimes called Michel Teroahauté in published accounts). Michel later went off with three other voyageurs, but returned alone to camp on 9 October 1821, claiming that the others were lost. It became increasingly obvious that Michel had killed the other three and had stowed the bodies nearby; he was using them as a private store of meat, occasionally sharing it with other hard-pressed members of the party. Then, on 20 October, Michel and Hood were sitting alone in a tent when a shot was heard. Hood was found to have been shot dead, though Michel claimed it was an accident. Richardson and Hepburn were now convinced that Michel intended to kill them one by one in order to eat them, and so on 23 October, Richardson – choosing his moment – shot Michel dead.

Against this backdrop of starvation, murder, cannibalism and extra-judicial execution, Franklin's expedition came to a conclusion as the remains of his party staggered into Fort Providence in December 1821. He had travelled over 5,500 miles on foot and by boat during some of the worst winter weather in living memory, and of his original party of 23, only five remained.

By any standards the expedition had been a disaster. Yet Franklin was promoted to commander in 1821, was made captain in 1822, and became one of the best-known figures in society. He published an account of the expedition, entitled *A Narrative of a Journey to the Shores of the Polar Sea in the Years 1819–22* (London, 1823), and came to be known as 'the man who ate his boots'.

In 1824 he approached the Admiralty with a plan for another survey of Canada's Arctic coast – an expedition duly sanctioned. Learning from bitter experience, he organised for stores to be laid in depots along his route, and between 1825 and 1827 he returned to Canada and ascended the MacKenzie River before heading out to sea, where he discovered and named Garry Island. The winter of 1825–26 passed quite pleasantly, as Franklin's base at Fort Franklin on the MacKenzie River had been well-provisioned. In the summer of 1826 he travelled north-westwards to Beechey Point, mapping over 400 miles of coastline, while other parties explored the Great Slave Lake and the area around Point Barrow. A second winter was passed at Fort Franklin, and he returned to Liverpool in September 1826.

Once more hailed a hero, he published a second book, *Narrative of a Second Expedition to the Shores of the Polar Sea in the Years 1825–27* (London, 1828). Knighted in 1829, he was made a Fellow of the Royal Geographical Society and the Geographical Society of Paris, and awarded an honorary doctorate by Oxford University. Further naval service in the Mediterranean preceded his appointment as lieutenant-governor of Tasmania (1836–43), an appointment that was punctuated by a series of disputes with both fellow government officials and members of the local population, and he was recalled in 1843.

The women in the life of this remarkable man were themselves remarkable. He married twice; firstly, in August 1823 he married Eleanor Anne Purden, a poet and woman of considerable intellect who played a prominent role in many learned societies. Having given birth to their first child, her health went into a sad decline, and she died on 22 February 1825 while Franklin was away in Canada.

In November 1828 he married Jane Griffin. The second Lady Franklin was an equally formidable character and had herself travelled widely. She would later visit Syria and Asia Minor, and would accompany her husband to Russia, Australia, New Zealand and Tasmania, where she became involved – perhaps too involved – in her husband's administration. She possessed an incredible resolve and would later ceaselessly bombard the Admiralty with demands that they search for her missing husband.

Franklin's second-in-command on his Northwest Passage expedition was Captain Francis Rawdon Moira Crozier, who took command of the expedition's second ship, the *Terror*. Born in 1796 in Banbridge, County Down, Crozier was an experienced polar explorer. He had served with Parry in the Arctic in 1821–23, and went on further expeditions in 1824 and 1827. In 1836 he travelled to Davis Strait with Sir James Clark Ross in search of missing whalers, and then took part in the Antarctic expedition of 1839–43. The two senior officers in this latest expedition were, then, highly experienced explorers. Yet Crozier had serious misgivings.

The Admiralty claimed that everything had been planned to the smallest detail, and asserted that three years' worth of provisions had been loaded aboard *Erebus* and *Terror*. Both ships were fitted with auxiliary steam engines, the first polar vessels to be so equipped. But the fitting of this steam machinery had reduced the amount of storage space available for food, while also increasing the draught of the ship and making navigation in shallow channels more difficult. Crozier was also aware that Franklin had never commanded a major sea expedition; he was an overland explorer and, if truth be told, a bad one at that. Finally, Crozier had just returned from a long expedition to the Antarctic and was exhausted.

Captain Francis Rawdon Crozier.

Erebus and Terror *sailing through pack ice during an 1842 expedition to Antarctica.*

But knowing that to refuse to take command of the *Terror* would be detrimental to his career, he agreed to go.

Franklin departed on 19 May 1845 with very specific instructions: he was to sail to Lancaster Sound and from there push westwards to Cape Walker. From Cape Walker, he was to strike southwards towards the Bering Strait. From their last port of call – on Disco Island, on the west coast of Greenland – the men of the expedition sent home cheerful letters, together with five of their number who had taken ill; these men would soon realise how lucky they had been. On 26 July in Melville Bay – as they waited to travel into Lancaster Sound – *Erebus* and *Terror* met up with two whaling ships, the *Enterprise* and the *Prince of Wales*. They stayed in contact with the whalers for a few days, and then drew away to the northeast, towards Lancaster Sound. It was the last time that Franklin, Crozier and the ships' crews of 127 men were seen alive.

CHAPTER FOUR

The First Searches

As early as 1846 doubts began to be raised as to the safety of the expedition, and the general public grew increasingly worried. But the Admiralty, confident that Franklin and his men were well-equipped and supplied, refused to send out search vessels. Franklin, one of the best-known explorers in the world, was travelling in an area he could consider his own backyard, having explored there – by land and by sea – on three previous occasions, and the Admiralty fully expected him to emerge into the Pacific having found a Northwest Passage. If his route was blocked by ice, he was expected to retrace his course back into the North Atlantic.

Though the official line remained optimistic,[11] no one knew if he was alive or dead. By 1847 officials at the Admiralty as well as the general public were beginning to realise that something had happened to Franklin and his men. The Admiralty hoped that his ships were merely beset by ice, and decided to send other ships to re-supply them. When relief plans were being drawn up in 1847 it was decided to follow three distinct courses of action:

  i) A sea expedition would sail to the north-west

coast of Alaska in the hope of meeting Franklin as he emerged from the Northwest Passage into the Pacific. The ships *Plover* and *Herald* would undertake this search.

ii) An overland expedition – led by Sir John Richardson and Dr John Rae – would explore the Arctic coast of Canada in the hope of finding traces of the expedition.

iii) A further sea expedition would follow Franklin's proposed course to Lancaster Sound and Cape Walker in the hope of finding his ships. For this expedition, HM Ships *Enterprise* and *Investigator* were put under the command of Sir James Clark Ross.

During the course of the next 30 years, over 40 expeditions would go to the Arctic in search of Franklin. These included Admiralty expeditions, overland parties sent out by the Hudson's Bay Company, and private expeditions funded through the efforts of Lady Franklin and others.

When it was announced that Sir James Clark Ross would lead a search expedition, many young officers rushed to join him; indeed, those wishing to volunteer far outnumbered the places available. McClintock was one of those who volunteered and was fortunate in that Captain Smyth, his old shipmate from the *Samarang*, recommended him to Ross.

Ross was a highly experienced Arctic explorer. In a polar career stretching back to 1818 he had taken part in six Arctic expeditions before taking command of *Erebus* and *Terror* in 1839 for an Antarctic expedition and an attempt on the magnetic South Pole. In 1842 he had led a second Antarctic expedition. Now, he insisted on taking command of the search expedition. A friend of both

Sir James Clarke Ross.

Franklin and Crozier, he had harboured doubts about the expedition since its inception. His uncle, Sir John Ross – also a polar explorer – sharing his misgivings about the expedition, had instructed Franklin to leave messages in stone cairns if he got into difficulties, and promised that he would press for a rescue mission if his return was delayed. Sir James Clark Ross was now confident that he could follow Franklin's projected course and find him and his men in the Arctic.

Ross would take two ships, the *Enterprise* and the *Investigator*, the latter being commanded by Captain Edward Joseph Bird. In February 1848 McClintock joined the crew of the *Enterprise* at Woolwich, and commenced duty as the ship's second officer. There were other Irish officers among the *Enterprise*'s crew; indeed, all of the watch officers had Irish connections. The first officer was Lieutenant Robert John Le Mesurier McClure, born in Wexford in 1807. He had joined the navy in 1824, and had previously travelled to the Arctic in the *Terror* as a member of Captain Sir George Back's expedition. McClure was an extremely strict disciplinarian and, while Ross curbed his worst excesses during this expedition, a later expedition of his own would end in near mutiny.

The third officer of the *Enterprise* was Lieutenant William ('Willy') Browne, the son of a Dublin harbour master. A talented artist who would later achieve some renown for his paintings of Arctic scenery, he had served in the merchant navy before joining the Royal Navy, and saw action in the First China War – or 'Opium War' – of 1839–41. This was his first experience of Arctic exploration.

Another Irish officer with the expedition was the assistant surgeon, Henry Mathias, born in Dublin in 1822. McClintock and Mathias soon struck up a firm friendship.

During the months of preparation prior to departure,

HM Ships Enterprise *and* Investigator –
the first ships to search for Franklin.

McClintock worked hard and gained invaluable experience of preparing for Arctic travel – experience that would serve him well in later years. Ross took him under his wing and imparted a wealth of Arctic knowledge. McClintock and Ross remained friends until Ross' death in 1861, and McClintock would often turn to him for advice.

In 1848 the various expeditions set out. *Plover* sailed on New Year's Day, and was to rendezvous with *Herald*, which was already operating in the Pacific. *Plover* was under the command of Thomas Moore, while *Herald* was commanded by Henry Kellett from Clonacody, County Tipperary – a man with a distinguished naval career behind him.[12] The searches undertaken by *Plover* and *Herald* were concentrated around the Bering Strait, but met with no success.

That same year, Dr (later Sir) John Richardson and Dr John Rae, of the Hudson's Bay Company, left England to carry out the land search in the area of the Great Slave Lake and the MacKenzie River. Dolphin and Union Strait was searched, as was the area around Cape Krusenstern. The party over-wintered at Fort Confidence before renewing its search in the spring of 1849. When Richardson returned to England in May 1849 Rae stayed on with a small group of volunteers, and in the 1850–51 seasons, travelled as far as Victoria Island, Prince Albert Sound and Pelly Point. He also searched the Kent Peninsula and Coronation Gulf, surveying over 630 miles of coastline. Though Rae found no traces of Franklin during these expeditions, he was convinced he was searching in the right area, and would later acquire the first solid intelligence as to the fate of the Franklin expedition.

In May 1848 *Enterprise* and *Investigator* sailed out of the Thames and headed northwards to the Arctic Circle. By 7 June they were off Cape Farewell, where McClintock saw pack ice for the first time. They crossed the Arctic Circle on 20 June, heading for the Whale Fish Islands, which they reached two days later. It was here that McClintock first met the Inuit, and he later described the encounter:

> They all came off to visit us, the men in their single canoes or kaiaks [*sic*], the women in a boat. They seemed a very well disposed quiet honest people, and when drawn out displayed a good deal of intelligence. They are good mimics, having a quick perception of one's salient points and are also very tolerable musicians. The people were all civilised and many of them mixed with the Danes; they spoke a few words of English. One man played the fiddle while the rest danced some jigs and

hornpipes picked up from the Danes. The
women also waltzed; the step was new to us
but they danced gracefully and kept remark-
ably good time. The men danced with much
greater spirit, throwing their arms about and
whisking the ladies round with much dexter-
ity. Everything they did was done with good
nature and showed a desire to please.[13]

McClintock was quick to recognise the usefulness of dog-
teams, and described how the Inuit used their dogs:

The dogs are invaluable as they scent out the
seal holes in the ice where the seals come to
breathe and they also draw the sledges. A good
team has drawn a loaded sledge 32 miles in four
hours, from one island to another over the sea.[14]

The expedition was following the route Franklin had been
ordered to take and, travelling along the west coast of
Greenland, McClintock observed not only the local wild-
life but also the habits of the indigenous Inuit.

By 20 August they had reached the northern end of
Baffin Bay; on 29 August they began sailing up Lancaster
Sound. Commanding a landing party, McClintock alighted
at Cape York where he came across a cairn of stones that
had been built by Ross in 1825. But not a trace of Franklin
could be found and no messages had been left behind.
Before rejoining the ships McClintock and his men built
a cairn of stones where he deposited a record.

Heavy pack ice now prevented *Enterprise* and *Investigator* from proceeding beyond Lancaster Sound. Finding
Barrow Strait and Prince Regent Inlet frozen from shore
to shore, Ross made the decision to over-winter at the

HM Ships Enterprise *and* Investigator
beset in the ice of Barrow Straits.

north-eastern end of North Somerset, at Port Leopold.
By September 1848 both ships had reached Port Leopold,
where they established their winter quarters. McClintock
and his shipmates would remain here until the following
spring, entombed in ice sustained by the sunless Arctic
winter. In October he recorded in his journal that they
had 'discontinued the practice of firing rockets and blue
lights at night', having concluded from the lack of
response that none of Franklin's men were in the immediate vicinity.

North Somerset – an island approximately 180 miles
long by 100 miles wide – was a desolate place. Nevertheless, previous Arctic expeditions had passed the winters
pleasantly, dispelling boredom and depression with
amateur theatre, music recitals, scientific lectures and
school lessons for the crew. Ross, though, had made no
preparations for such activities, and the men were left

to pass the time as best they could. Cramped in miserable conditions, the sunless days passed slowly, prompting some members of the crews to their own efforts at alleviating the boredom. Edward White, the clerk aboard the *Enterprise*, organised lessons for the illiterate, while one of the master's mates gave instruction on navigation. McClintock occupied himself with his reading, going through both scientific texts and accounts of previous expeditions.

Some relief was afforded on 30 November when they celebrated St Andrew's Day. McClintock noted in his journal:

> St. Andrew's Day – in commemoration of the patron saint of Scotland, Sir James dined with us. On disclosing our nationality, we discovered our party to consist of four Irishmen [McClintock, McClure, Browne and Mathias], two Scotch [*sic*] [Sir James and Robinson] and one English [Biggs]. An unusual preponderance of Irish for the Navy.[15]

Christmas and New Year were also occasions of celebration, as was St Patrick's Day 1849, when McClintock wrote of how Kellett had

> Landed his new sledge – the *Eriu* – out upon the floe down an inclined place from the ship's side during our absence and we saw her laying there in that state, with her green banner flying, on our return. The Carpenter was launched on the *Eriu* and her crew having cheered loudly, were given a bottle of porter each to drink success to her.[16]

Otherwise, life was a grim affair as the crews eked out an

existence aboard ships whose interiors were coated with ice caused by the freezing of the condensation of their breath. McClintock described the efforts to deal with it:

> The lower deck is very damp, constant wiping is necessary as the beams and bulkhead in a short time becomes dripping wet. This occupation serves for the 'Cripple Gang' as the invalids are called, and is a preparatory step to returning them to their duties upon deck.[17]

For the majority of the crew, this was a period of wretched discomfort – a miserable winter during which two crewmen passed away.

By late February 1849 the sun was beginning to return; the temperature, however, remained at around -49°F. Preparations got underway for the following season's exploration, and the ships' crews were ordered to commence cutting the vessels from the ice. A small hut and supply depot were established at Whaler Point, and these would be essential for the two sledging parties Ross intended to send out. Lieutenant Browne would lead one party southwards from Port Leopold to Fury Beach, an area visited by Parry during his 1821–23 expedition aboard the *Fury*, and where he had deposited stores. Ross was anxious to learn if Franklin had landed there to replenish his own stores; if so, it was hoped he had left a message regarding his intentions. While Browne headed south (he was to reach Prince Regent Inlet), Ross would lead his own sledging party to the northwest of the island, accompanied by McClintock. It was to be an epic trip.

Throughout spring, preparations were made. They would take two sledges with crews of six men each, one sledge under the command of Ross, the other led by

McClintock. Having observed the Inuit mode of travel on Greenland, they endeavoured to make their preparations in accordance with native practice. Yet they had brought no sledge-dogs and would have to rely on man-hauling, something that the Inuit would never do. McClintock, innovative in other areas, experimented with methods of cooking, and organised a system using spirit lamps and kettles. For the remainder of his career, he would seek to improve methods of overland travel. Ultimately, he would be recognised as the father of modern sledging techniques.

The proposed sledging expeditions represented a giant leap forward in the history of polar exploration. Previously, sledge crews had explored only the small areas close to where they landed or over-wintered. This was the first occasion on which parties set out to explore a large area and which necessitated a prolonged absence from their ships. McClintock later wrote:

> On the 15th May 1849, the first of the sledging parties set out upon the Franklin search, from the expedition under the command of Captain Sir James C. Ross, then wintering in Port Leopold, lat. 74° N., long. 90° W. Since that time nearly a hundred such parties have been dispatched from the various expeditions wintering in the Arctic regions, and have travelled upwards of 40,000 miles in the same search; yet, when I look back upon this first pioneering journey, productive as it was of such inconsiderable results, my respect for it continues unabated, since we underwent as much privation and fatigue as in any equal period of my subsequent travel. In the fitting

out of our two sledges we availed ourselves
of all the experience of former expeditions:
each was drawn by six men; upon each we
placed thirty days' rations and a tent; and
provisions were forwarded by other parties
upon our route.[18]

He continued:

Sir James Ross led the party and I had the
good fortune to accompany; we remained
absent the unprecedented period of forty days,
accomplishing a distance of 500 miles. Seven
of our twelve men returned in comparative
health; the other five having quite broken
down under the fatigue.[19]

When the sledging parties set out they were pulled
by an enlarged party of 24 men. With McClintock following in his path, Ross led the way, directing the sledges
along the easiest route. Travelling mostly by night, the
daily march usually ended at 5am, when the tents were
pitched, supper served and the men would rest until
around 5pm. McClintock later described the party's living
conditions on the march:

Our arrangements for the journey were very
simple: our tents covered a space of 6 feet by
9 – just room enough for seven persons to lie
down in. Our tent furniture consisted of a
waterproof floor-cloth, a blanket bag for each
person and a couple of furs, one to spread
underneath and the other over us. We travelled by night and slept by day, for the double

reason of avoiding the intense noonday snow glare, and of travelling during the hours when it was too cold to sleep in our tent.[20]

By 20 May they had reached Garnier Bay. Having established a depot, the supply parties returned to the ships. Ross and McClintock travelled on with the sledging parties and, en route, a point between Port Leopold and Garnier Bay was christened Cape McClintock – the first geographical feature to be named after him. They continued further west before turning south. North Somerset was, at this time, largely unexplored, and vital survey work was undertaken along the way. On 26 May they reached Cape Bunny. Previously sighted by Parry in 1819, he believed it to be a promontory of North Somerset, but Ross discovered it was an island separated from North Somerset by a narrow channel.

From Cape Bunny, the expedition continued south, crossing the frozen inlet between Cape Pressure and Cape Granite. Battling through ridges of hummocked ice, they reached Four Rivers Bay on 6 June. About 50 miles to the south, they could see a previously unknown coast, christened Cape Bird by Ross. Along their route they had found many fossils and a number of abandoned Inuit camps. McClintock wrote:

> Near the river in Transition Valley ruins of a few summer huts of the Esquimaux were seen; i.e. the circles of stones which had been used to keep down the sides of their skin tents. Also, to the south of Cape Pressure, we found ruins of a few winter and several summer abodes; portions of the bones of four whales lay about, and we dug up the side of a wooden sledge.[21]

The sledge parties had by this time reached the limit to which they could safely travel, and Ross and McClintock agreed they should return to the ships. Before they left Four Rivers Bay, a cairn was erected and a record deposited in it. In addition, a depot of supplies was established for the use of Franklin and his men, should they happen upon them. But little did Ross and McClintock realise how close they were to solving the Franklin mystery. The evidence of Franklin's ultimate fate lay further south, near Cape Bird, and it would be another ten years before McClintock would make his discovery.

As the sledging parties returned north, a shortage of food became apparent. During the outward journey, a large supply of fresh meat had been obtained by shooting birds. Using the skills he had learned as a young man while out shooting with his father around Dundalk, McClintock had managed to shoot over twenty birds, which were stewed and eaten. On the return journey, however, birds were found to be in short supply, and McClintock only managed to shoot birds on three occasions, each man being allotted half a bird. Strength began to fail and one man had to be carried on the sledge. McClintock later described the journey back to the ships:

> This harassing journey greatly knocked up our men; indeed, their strength had latterly been greatly impaired, inasmuch that they were utterly unable to lengthen their journeys beyond the outward bound ones, although our sledges had become greatly lightened. The recent fall of snow not only augmented the difficulty of travel, but had also almost obliterated our former track, by which it was desirable we should return through this rough

hummocky ice. Nor was it the only evil it occa-
sioned; for, owing to the uniform dazzling
whiteness of the surface, and the total absence
of sun to throw any, even the faintest shadow,
it was necessary to strain our eyes in every
direction, at the expense of much pain, and
the risk of bringing snow blindness.[22]

He continued:

> The men seem much weakened, and have the
> most ravenous appetites. I do not exagger-
> ate when I say that they could devour at least
> three times their allowance without incon-
> venience; and I think double allowance could
> it possibly be spared, would not by any means
> be too much for them. Not a drop of water
> could be found amongst the rocks where we
> procured a small supply on the 31st of May,
> the recent severe weather having thoroughly
> frozen the water in all the pools.[23]

Totally exhausted and famished with hunger, they
reached the ships on 23 June. The expedition had lasted
39 days, during which more than 500 miles had been travelled – the longest sledge journey ever completed by an
expedition, and one which had discovered and charted
a large area of North Somerset.

It was obvious that mistakes had been made in the
journey's preparation. The ration allowance was too low
and the men had been asked to haul too much – facts
carefully noted by McClintock, who believed that if sledging techniques could be improved and a more efficient
way of cooking developed, sledge travel would become

the most effective way of exploring the polar regions. He could take personal satisfaction from emerging quite well from the expedition. On their return to the ships, Ross took to his bed, while all the others were put on the sick-list; only McClintock remained fit for duty. He would emerge from subsequent expeditions in good health, though it must be pointed out that he led his sledge teams in the literal sense – unlike later explorers, he did not stand in the traces and pull with the men. For a Victorian naval officer, this would have been unthinkable. Many years later, he wrote of the hardships of the expedition with Sir James Clark Ross:

> Out of the twelve picked men by whom the two sledges were drawn, five were completely knocked up, and every man required a consid-erable time under medical care to recruit his strength after this lengthened period of intense labour, constant exposure and insuf-ficient food.[24]

Any triumph McClintock may have felt in the season's successes was immediately dispelled by tragic news. His closest friend on the *Enterprise*, Henry Mathias, had been ailing since the spring and, coughing up blood, had grown gradually weaker. It appears Mathias realised he would not recover and, on 2 June 1849, drew up his will. Two weeks later he was dead.

In his journal, McClintock described the death of another of the ship's crew:

> Poor James Gray, seaman, had died in our absence. He had been gradually sinking for three months. His malady was originally more

mental than physical. From being one of the most cheerful of our crew, he became desponding and melancholily [sic] fancied himself ill and convinced himself that he could not live to reach England. Eventually the mind subdued the body. He became really ill and sank rapidly under it. He died without pain and was, I believe, prepared for another world; the assistant surgeon having daily read prayers to him from time to time before his death. With great labour a grave was dug ashore, beside that of poor Combes [sic], a carpenter of the *Investigator* who died last autumn.[25]

Ross had fully intended to renew exploring later in the summer, but scurvy began to appear among the ships' crews. Out of a crew of 64 aboard the *Enterprise*, twelve men were placed on the sick-list due to scurvy. Before long, both Ross and McClure were ill, and command devolved to McClintock. He began the work of cutting the ships free, taking out land and boat parties to saw through the ice, which ranged in thickness from 3–5 feet. He also organised shooting parties to provide fresh meat for the sick. By 17 August McClure was off the sick-list and able to assume command. By the end of August, *Enterprise* and *Investigator* had broken free from the ice.

There was still some of the navigable season remaining and Ross intended to search Barrow Strait and Melville Island. Yet, beset again by ice, the ships were carried southwards down Lancaster Sound. A second winter trapped in the ice – and with it, the possibility of death by scurvy – now seemed likely. On 24 September, however, with the ships held fast by the freezing grip of Baffin Bay, the ice began to break up. Given the state of the crews' health, Ross wisely decided to use this opportunity to head for home.

On reaching the western coast of Greenland, a party went ashore at Wolstenholme Sound. Here, McClintock found deserted Inuit huts and counted the bodies of fourteen Inuit men, women and children. He pondered the possible cause of death. Was it starvation, or had they come into contact with Europeans and been infected with some disease? Among the scattered debris, he found evidence of the presence of Europeans – nails, an empty meat can and canvas bearing government insignia. This, he deduced, indicated that these Inuit had been in contact with the crew of the supply ship, the *North Star*, or with men from Franklin's expedition.

On 5 November 1849 *Enterprise* and *Investigator* sailed into Scarborough. Their return, however, was tinged with regret as they learnt that there was still no word of Franklin and his men. The crews were paid off later in the month, and McClintock and his shipmates went on well-earned leave.

In a lecture to the Royal Dublin Society in 1856 McClintock expressed his regrets about the expedition, which centred chiefly on their failure to explore further towards Cape Bird:

> Following the shores of North Somerset to its western extremity, Cape Bunny (which we discovered to be an island), we found that broad strait leading southwards intervened between us and Cape Walker. Hence, Sir James wisely determined to depart from his original intention of travelling to the westward, for the purpose of exploring this newly found strait. Following the western slopes of North

Somerset, we endeavoured to traverse the whole of the unknown space intervening between it and the Magnetic Pole, in lat. 70° N., long. 97° W. Our failure was doubly unfortunate, 1st, because we were marching in the right direction, as the discoveries of Dr Rae in 1854 have proved; and 2ndly, because a *magnetic* attraction in that quarter was most uncharitably attributed to our leader who, it will be remembered, discovered the Magnetic Pole some eighteen years before. It is not to be wondered that the succeeding expeditions were shy of attempting anything in that unpopular direction; hence, it remains to this hour the only unexplored area of the easily accessible portion of the Arctic regions. It may not be out of place, perhaps, to remark that it was within sight of the Magnetic Pole that some forty or fifty of Franklin's crews were seen by the Esquimaux in the spring of 1850, dragging a boat to the southward, and the remains of which boat have since been found within the estuary of the Great Fish River.[26]

On the navigability of Peel Sound, he wrote:

Our opinion of the strait [Peel Sound], which we had discovered was, that any attempt to force a ship down it would not only fail, but lead to almost inevitable risk of destruction, in consequence of it being choked up with heavy ice. My subsequent experience had led me to modify this opinion. In 1849 we travelled down along the leeward side of the strait, where all the ice pressure was most apparent and striking; but in 1851 Lieut. Browne travelled down the windward side, and found the ice smooth, so much so as to show that water must have existed the previous autumn nearly all along the western shore. Moreover, it is now almost beyond a doubt, that Franklin's ships did pass down it in 1846.[27]

Yet the realisation of these facts lay many years in the future. For now, McClintock was content to have taken part in an epic sledge trip during which he gained valuable experience while working alongside Ross, a giant of polar exploration. Now developing his own theories on Arctic travel, McClintock had emerged from this first expedition unscathed and unfazed – remarkable, given that many explorers of the period never returned to the Arctic after experiencing its dangers and hardships. This ability to survive and adapt would become a hallmark of Leopold McClintock's career.

CHAPTER FIVE

HMS Assistance

Ross, Bird, McClure and McClintock had no sooner returned with the *Enterprise* and *Investigator* when the two ships were refitted and dispatched, via South America, to the Bering Strait. *Enterprise* was under the command of Captain Richard Collinson, and the newly promoted Commander McClure had charge of *Investigator*. Unfortunately, the two ships lost contact following a storm in the Strait of Magellan, and – as with the previous expeditions – this latest search for Franklin was to prove fruitless.[28]

McClintock had gone home to Ireland following his return from the Arctic in November 1849. He found his homeland much changed, devastated as it was by the Famine of the 1840s. Nevertheless, he spent his leave engaged in study, developing his theories on Arctic navigation and sledge travel.

The Admiralty soon announced that more search vessels were being sent to the Arctic. Captain Horatio Austin was to lead an expedition comprised of the *Resolute* and *Assistance*, assisted by two tenders, the *Pioneer* and *Intrepid*. At the same time, a fleet of smaller brigs and tenders was organised under the command of Sir John

Ross; his fleet consisted of the *Lady Franklin*, HMS *Sophia* and the *Felix*. Lady Franklin herself also commissioned a search, employing the schooner *Prince Albert* under Commander Charles Forsyth. A further expedition – comprised of the brigs, *Advance* and *Rescue*, under the command of Lieutenant Edwin De Haven USN (United States Navy) – was dispatched by the American merchant, Henry Grinnell. In 1850 then, no less than eleven ships headed to the Arctic with the intention of searching the Wellington Channel.

McClintock soon became involved in this veritable frenzy of activity, being appointed first lieutenant aboard the *Assistance*. The ship was to be commanded in the Arctic by Captain Erasmus Ommanney,[29] who had served in the Arctic with Sir James Clark Ross in 1836 during an expedition in search of missing whalers reported to be beset by ice in Davis Strait. Crozier – Franklin's second-in-command – had served on the same expedition. Willy Browne – McClintock's shipmate from the *Enterprise* and *Investigator* expedition – was also signed up for this latest search, serving as second lieutenant aboard *Resolute*.

McClintock threw himself into the organisation of the expedition, seeing to the stowing of provisions aboard *Assistance* – enough for three years. Though Captain Austin had previously served in the Arctic – aboard the *Fury* in 1824–25 – he had not taken part in any long-distance sledging expeditions, and therefore depended on McClintock to organise supplies and equipment for the planned sledging trips. Privately, McClintock was hoping to make a sledge journey of at least 700 miles.

It was during this preparatory period that McClintock became acquainted with Lady Franklin. She immediately recognised his potential as an explorer and would later turn to him when organising another private expedition.

HM Ships Intrepid, Assistance, Resolute *and* Pioneer –
sent in search of Franklin.

In late April 1850 the ships went down to Greenhithe,
where they were visited by Sir Edward Parry, the venerable Arctic explorer, before heading out to sea. Passing
Cape Farewell, they encountered strong winds and icebergs, and reached Whale Fish Islands on 15 June 1850,
where supplies were replenished. On resumption, the
expedition struggled towards Melville Bay.

The intention was to travel northwards through Baffin
Bay as far as Melville Bay, at the mouth of Lancaster Sound.
This was made extremely difficult due to the southerly
current which then prevailed in Baffin Bay, and which
caused the bay and Davis Strait to be clogged with icebergs
and floes. This vast body of ice, known as the 'middle pack',
could travel at considerable speeds as it was swept along
by the current. The bay was a navigator's nightmare, and
it took skill and determination to avoid being beset in the
ice and being swept out of the bay altogether. It was not

Officers who took part in the Franklin search expeditions, l–r: Osborn (Pioneer), Allard (Pioneer), McClintock (Intrepid), Pullen (North Star), Richards (Assistance).

uncommon for ships to be smashed apart by the fast-flowing bergs – in 1830 alone, nineteen ships had been destroyed while trying to pass through Baffin Bay. The *Resolute* and *Assistance*, however, had the advantage of having auxiliary steam power, and by 1 July had reached the edge of Melville Bay. There, they found a fleet of whaling ships waiting for the more favourable conditions that would allow them to attempt Lancaster Sound, and the expedition similarly decided to await better weather. During this interval, boat parties went to the nearby Vrouw Islands to explore and to shoot birds. McClintock was a participant in these trips, and shot many birds that were then dried and stored to provide meat for later in the voyage.

That summer of 1850 was especially harsh, and though many of the whalers headed south through Davis Strait – abandoning hope of clearing Lancaster Sound due to the density of the pack ice – the rescue parties were obliged to remain. McClintock navigated *Assistance* as it tried various leads in an attempt to find a way out of Melville Bay, but by 7 July the pressure of the southward-flowing ice was so severe that an ice dock had to be cut. Here, *Assistance* sheltered, together with a whaler, the *True Love*. *Resolute* and the various tenders also sought the safety of ice docks. Later, when the southerly flow of pack abated to some degree, McClintock and his men would have to labour to cut the ship free.

Throughout this period, they were surrounded by the fantastic shapes created by the pressure of the Arctic ice. Vast pillars of ice rose upwards, only to disappear in an instant when the terrific pressure blew the bergs asunder with an ear-splitting crash. Illuminated by the rays of the midnight sun, McClintock led hunting parties out over the ice floes in search of fresh meat.

The environment was totally hostile; on 12 July the ice closed in and *Assistance* began to be 'nipped' by the ice. The ship was pushed upwards 3 feet by the ice, and there was an anxious wait before it would be known if she could stand the pressure. Should the press of ice become too much she would be crushed, and the crew would be marooned on the ice to await rescue by *Resolute* and the other tenders. McClintock later wrote:

> The straining and cracking of the ship's timbers was not a pleasant sound, but when I saw that the floes were firmly set against each other, ahead and astern of the ship, and that she had risen to the pressure, I felt quite satisfied of our safety. The young people seemed to enjoy the excitement of the scene without appearing to understand the danger, and were

only anxious to know whether this was really
a good nip. With the tenders the pressure was
more severe. A little more and they must both
have been destroyed. Shortly before midnight
the ice slacked, and allowed the ship to settle
down to her usual draft of water.[30]

The small squadron of ships remained trapped in this
pack ice until 17 July, when the pressure finally slackened.
The smaller tenders, however, were encased in a floe that
began to drift southwards, and they were only extricated
with difficulty. The expedition was obliged to blast its way
through the ice field, opening leads by using charges of
gunpowder. Finally, by 9 August, the small flotilla of ships
had succeeded in cutting, blasting and barging its way
into the 'North Water' of Baffin Bay. They had spent 45
days trying to find a route out of Melville Bay.

On southern Greenland, the expedition acquired
sledge-dogs and a dog-driver – an interpreter named Carl
Petersen, who would later accompany McClintock on the
Fox expedition. At Fort York, they met Inuit, described
by Sir John Ross after his encounter with them in 1818 as
'Arctic Highlanders'. Marvellously adapted to the climate,
they were accomplished hunters. One of their number –
named Kallihirua – was persuaded to join the expedition.

There was disturbing news at Fort York: Sir John Ross'
interpreter, Adam Beck, was told by the Inuit that two
ships had been wrecked on that coast and that all the
crew members had died. A series of searches could find
no evidence of these wrecks, and ultimately it would
become clear that these shipwrecks were not those of
Franklin and his men. Now, as the Arctic winter drew near,
McClintock and his shipmates knew they must quickly
establish their winter quarters.

CHAPTER SIX

Winter Preparations

As the weather worsened the flotilla of ships made for Lancaster Sound with the intention of establishing winter quarters. Battling through severe gales and heavy seas, landing parties went ashore to survey spots where Franklin and his men may have landed during their voyage through Lancaster Sound. At Cape Riley the first evidence of Franklin's presence was discovered when the remains of a campsite was found. Evidently, some of Franklin's men had come ashore here for a hunting expedition and to collect scientific samples. Some members of the current expedition interpreted this as evidence that Franklin had retreated this way en route to Pond's Bay, in the hope of meeting whaling ships. McClintock was not convinced. The scattered debris at Cape Riley was too old, and he felt sure it was evidence of Franklin passing through Lancaster Sound at the commencement of his expedition. He was also convinced that Franklin's crews had spent their first winter in the vicinity, and McClintock hoped to find their winter quarters and perhaps a message regarding Franklin's further intentions.

McClintock felt that, had he been in Franklin's position, he would have chosen to over-winter on Beechey

Island, and he pressed for a thorough search of the island. Captain Austin, however, wanted to search Cape Hotham at the western end of Wellington Channel. The *Assistance* sailed past Beechey Island, leaving its search to the crews of *Resolute* and *Pioneer*. McClintock's theories regarding Franklin's movements proved to be correct when the search parties found the remains of his first winter quarters – there was a great deal of debris scattered on Beechey Island. Ominously, three graves were also found – those of John Hartnell and William Braine of *Erebus*, and John Torrington of *Terror*. Despite an exhaustive search, no written record was found.

McClintock now began to fear the worst. It was five years since the crews of *Terror* and *Erebus* had last been seen alive. They had only carried enough provisions for three years, but if rations had been supplemented by hunting, it would have been conceivable that some of Franklin's men were still alive. Yet here was evidence of men dying in their first Arctic winter. It did not bode well.

Assistance carried on westwards through Wellington Channel until it became beset in the ice off Barlow Inlet, on the coast of Cornwallis Island. Breaking free again, Cape Hotham was rounded, where large fields of fast-moving bergs were encountered. The *Assistance* was hit by several large bergs and, by 7 September, the ship – together with *Resolute*, *Intrepid* and *Pioneer* – was beset by ice off the shore of Griffith Island. Captain Penny and Sir John Ross took shelter in Assistance Harbour while the American vessels turned for home. As the pack ice gradually froze solid around them, the ships' crews prepared to endure the Arctic winter.

Having experienced a bleak winter with Sir James Clark Ross in 1848–49, McClintock and his shipmates made great efforts to ensure that this winter would pass more pleasantly. The men were issued with extra winter clothing, including flannel-lined trousers and jacket, a seal-skin cap and gloves, and stout boots. Great care was taken with the men's rations, and little luxuries, such as Australian tinned beef and apples, were issued, while fresh bread was baked and beer brewed.

McClintock was well aware of how the inactivity imposed by the Arctic winter could sap morale and cause depression. He encouraged the men to undertake expeditions to Griffith Island, and classes in mathematics and navigation were held. Both *Assistance* and *Resolute* published journals – *Assistance* issued the *Aurora Borealis* while *Resolute* put out the *Arctic Illustrated News*. McClintock contributed three articles to the *Aurora Borealis* and, with the other officers, planned further entertainments for the men. The nights of Christmas 1850 and New Year's Day 1851 were occasions for massive celebrations, but the great triumph of that winter was the Arctic theatre. Early in November McClintock – assisted by the ship's carpenter, William Dean – commenced the construction of an ad hoc theatre aboard *Assistance*. Willy Browne came over from *Resolute* to paint the theatrical backdrops and design a series of play bills, and during the course of the winter, plays, comedies, dances and masqued balls were held. The officers and men all played a role, acting both male and female parts – indeed, so convincing were the female leads, the young Inuit (now christened Erasmus York) afterwards spent days searching the ship for these 'women'. Both Austin and Ommanney played the occasional role, but McClintock appeared on stage only once, and even then was hidden behind a mask.

In addition to organising these festivities, McClintock was also engaged in making preparations for the following season's sledging operations. Captain Austin, totally inexperienced in these matters, left all the details to his first lieutenant, who had learned much from his previous sledging experience with Ross. McClintock knew that they must start out early in the season – some time in April. He also understood the importance of establishing supply depots along the proposed route, and in October 1850 led a sledge party of seven men with the intention of laying a depot in the direction of Melville Island. They travelled over the ice for four days, enduring temperatures of -13°F, and eventually established a depot around 30 miles from the ship. This was the first time that sledge travel in the autumn had been carried out.

As the sun slowly returned, March 1851 proved to be the coldest month, the men enduring temperatures as low as -53°F. Early in 1851 a committee of the ships' officers and heads of department was given responsibility for organising the sledging equipment. In reality, McClintock had already formed his plans while on leave in Dublin in 1849, and had made lists of the necessary equipment and supplies. Ten and six-man sledges were built to his specifications, and packed with tents, wolf and buffalo-skin sleeping robes, blankets and waterproof floor coverings. When fully loaded, each sledge would weigh just over 1,300 pounds.

Having experienced cooking difficulties when travelling with Ross, McClintock intended to use a spirit lamp to heat kettles and pots; the Arctic was no place to cook over an open fire. Recalling the difficulties endured on North Somerset in 1849, when food had run low during the return to the ship, he paid special attention to the men's rations. Each man was allocated a generous daily allowance, including simple luxuries such as tobacco and rum. The men were also issued additional clothing, including cotton jumpers, warm socks and canvas boots.

Sledge parties departing from Resolute *and* Intrepid *to search for Franklin.*

McClintock intended to carry out the most extensive search to date for Franklin and his missing men, and was determined to maximise the distance he could travel from the ship. He organised support parties to accompany the main sledges, as this would enable him to travel over 350 miles from the ships. On the return journey, he would use depots that had been established along his route.

Fifteen sledges set out from the ships, and throughout March 1851 McClintock put the men through their paces, during which they practised using kites and sails to help pull the sledges – ideas that would later have some success.

The key question was where to search. Though Beechey Island was searched in 1850, and North Somerset had been searched in 1849, vast stretches of the Arctic had yet to be searched. Captain Penny was directed to search Wellington Channel, while three parties under Captain Ommanney would search in the direction of Cape Walker.

*McClintock's sledge parties experimented
with kites and sails to help pull sledges.*

In addition, smaller parties would search the islands to the west. The longest journey would be to Melville Island – a trip left to McClintock, the most experienced sledge traveller in the expedition.

On 4 April 1851 the first sledge party set out to explore the channel between Bathurst Island and Cornwallis Island. Depots had been laid down there in autumn, and now it was intended to ascertain if they had been opened by survivors of Franklin's expedition.

The other sledges set out on 15 April, each having been given a name, a motto and a flag. Ommanney's sledge was christened *Reliance*, and Sherard Osborn's *True Belief*. McClintock's flag was a blue cross on a white field, his sledge named *Perseverance*, his motto, 'Persevere to the end' – apt, given that McClintock and his team were about to embark on the longest sledge journey yet taken.

CHAPTER SEVEN

North to Melville Island

A new chapter in the history of Arctic exploration commenced on 15 April 1851 when fourteen sledges, crewed by 102 men, assembled on the north-west bluff of Griffith Island. This was to be the starting point for a series of sledging expeditions which would rate as the most ambitious programme of Arctic land travel as yet undertaken.

The various sledge crews and their support parties were to head out in different directions to search for signs of the Franklin expedition. McClintock, the most experienced overland traveller in the expedition, would explore Melville Island – a round journey of about 80 days. Aside from undertaking the longest journey yet, he had several theories he wished to prove. Parry had over-wintered at Melville Island in 1819–20. Bushnan Cove, on the west side of the island, was a sheltered location, and had been described by Parry in his book, *Journal of a voyage for the discovery of a North West Passage in the years 1819–20* (London, 1821), as a suitable winter harbour and a good place for game. McClintock was convinced that if Franklin had wintered in this area, he would have stayed at Bushnan Cove – a hypothesis he was now intent on testing.

Hoping to travel there at a rate of 10 miles per day, McClintock later described the beginning of the outward journey:

> My journey had for its object the search of the southern shores of Melville Island, where Parry, in 1819, for the first time braved an Arctic winter, and which he describes as a favourite resort of reindeer and musk-ox. In short, we considered it as an Arctic paradise. Great was my joy, and unbounded was the enthusiasm of my men: not only did they expect to find our missing countrymen there, but also to enjoy an unlimited supply of venison steaks. Melville Island, however, was nearly 300 miles away, and to reach it difficulties had to be surmounted. In overcoming them my party proved themselves to be all that I could wish, and deserving of my highest commendations. The first check to our exuberant spirits came in the shape of frost-bites. The temperature suddenly fell to 40° below zero, the mercury froze, and a gale was blowing. To ascertain the extent of injury, it was necessary to examine the men's feet, ten out of thirty-five men were rendered unserviceable, and sent back to the ships. I shall never forget the anxious entreaties of some of these men to be allowed to continue the journey; when they found they could not conceal from me their wounds, they shed tears like children, as they parted from us upon their dreary homeward march.[31]

McClintock's sledge team was made up of *Resolute*'s

surgeon, Abraham R. Bradford, a number of seamen –
James Wilkie, James Hoile, John Salmon – and two
marines – Thomas Hood and Jim Heels. Some of these
men had served previously with McClintock aboard HMS
Enterprise. As they set out they were shadowed by Bob
Aldrich and his team, and a support sledge commanded
by Dicky Pearse. They travelled between 6pm and 6am,
trudging through the night and resting by day in order
to avoid the heat and glare of the sun and, with it, the
danger of snow-blindness. Despite travelling in the
improving spring weather, they still faced extremely harsh
conditions. McClintock later wrote:

> April 24th. Wind gradually freshening, frost-
> bites constantly playing about the men's faces.
> Scarcely was one cheek restored to circulation
> when the other would be caught. Too cold to
> lunch, so we hastened on in the hope of
> getting shelter from the land, but in this we
> were disappointed. The weather became too
> severe to proceed, and Mr S., having lost sensa-
> tion in both his great toes (although he had
> been dragging his sledge with his utmost
> strength without intermission), we were
> obliged to encamp at midnight, when only
> half-way across the bay. It blew with unabated
> fury all day, coming down off the high land
> in violent squalls; dense clouds of snow-drift
> drove past, and the weather extremely cold
> and cheerless. Temp 27° below zero. During
> the gale our little tent was very cold, and the
> steam of cooking, together with the moisture
> of our breath, condensed in considerable quan-
> tity on the inside, so that each flap caused a

shower of fine snow to fall over us, penetrat-
ing and wetting our blanket-bags. We all felt
delighted to be again on the march, after our
twenty-three hours' detention in tents 8ft. 8
in. long by 6 ft. 6 in. wide; in this space seven
of us were packed. At these low temperatures
(18° to 25° below zero) the fat of our salt pork
becomes hard and brittle like suet; to drink
out of a pannikin without leaving the skin of
one's lips attached to it, requires considerable
experience and caution; the small tin water-
bottles carried by the men in their breasts
were generally frozen after an hour or two.[32]

Every piece of metal had become a potential danger.
Without care, lips would freeze to canteens when taking
a drink or hands would freeze to metal tools when gloves
were not worn. The handles and eyepieces of McClintock's
sextant had to be coated with leather to ensure he could
take navigational sightings in safety.

During this expedition McClintock experimented with
different methods of pulling the sledge. He later wrote:

We often derived assistance from our tent
'floorcloth', set as a sail upon the sledge – the
tent poles serving as mast and yard. In this
manner we travelled to Liddon's Gulf, in a very
thick fog, before a fresh, fair wind, with the
addition of a large kite, which not only gave
us a friendly pull, but served to guide us whenever the land was obscured from view.[33]

At the end of each day's march, at 6am, the men had
supper, usually consisting of pemmican, biscuits and a

tot of grog. To supplement food and fuel McClintock shot at any game that crossed his path. He later described how a polar bear came close to their camp:

> Shortly after pitching our tents, a bear was seen approaching. The guns were prepared, men called in, and perfect silence maintained in our little camp. The animal approached from the leeward, taking advantage of every hummock to cover his advance until within seventy yards; then, putting himself in a sitting posture, he pushed forward with his hind-legs, steadying his body with his fore-legs out-stretched. In this manner he advanced for about ten yards further, stopped a minute or two intently eyeing our encampment, and snuffling the air in evident doubt; then he commenced a retrograde movement by pushing himself backwards with his fore-legs as he had previously advanced with the hinder ones. As soon as he presented his shoulder, Mr Bradford and I fired, breaking a leg and other-wise wounding him severely; but it was not until he had got 300 yards off, and had received six bullets, that we succeeded in killing him. All the fat and blubber amounted only to about 50 lbs. This, together with some choice bear-steaks, we took. His stomach contained portions of seal.[34]

A few days later McClintock shot another bear, and would later shoot a musk ox, some hares and birds. He had studied Inuit hunting methods, and often used a white cloth shield to approach game in order to make his shot.

*Stuffed polar bear donated by McClintock
to Dublin's Natural History Museum.*

In light of dwindling polar-bear numbers, most people today would disapprove of killing these creatures except where human life is endangered. In the context of a mid-nineteenth-century overland expedition, however, these animals represented a vital source of food and fuel.[35]

On 29 April he bade farewell to the crew of his support sledge, and his own party trudged onwards in the direction of Melville Island, McClintock scouting ahead to find easy routes across the ice fields or through the hummocked ice.

On 11 May Bradford's party broke off from the main group in order to explore the east coast of Melville Island. McClintock later described how such partings inspired feelings of loneliness in both groups:

> It was here that I separated from the sledge 'Resolute', under the command of Mr Bradford, on the 11th of May, in order that he might explore the east coast, whilst I searched the south shore of Melville Island; he had been my excellent companion for twenty-five days of anxious outward journeying. After his departure I could only give vent to my reflections by inscribing them in my diary, and at once wrote down this passage: 'When our isolated position is considered, how completely we are exposed to all the vicissitudes of a rigorous climate, and dependent on our own efforts, and the accidental condition of the ice for advance or retreat, had not hope come to the rescue, our farewell would have indeed been a painful one'. That Bradford felt something of this sort is evident from the passage in his diary: 'We shook hands and wished each other success.

I must admit that when the "Perseverance" [McClintock's sledge] was lost sight of in the distance, I began to have some little feeling of the loneliness of our position, almost as if the last link connecting us with the living world had been severed. That these feelings were participated in by the men of the two parties, was evidenced by the manner in which they cheered and shook hands with each other.'[36]

McClintock and his men passed along the coast of Bathurst Island, sighted by Parry in 1819–20. Though this was the first time Europeans had walked along this coast, McClintock noted evidence of Inuit activity:

Encamped near the south extreme [Cape Gillman] . . . Found here a number of flat stones on a gravel ridge close to the beach, with several bones around them. Amongst these were the skull of a musk-ox, antler of a deer, and jaw of a bear. This was plainly the site of an Esquimaux encampment.[37]

Aldrich's party now broke off to explore Bathurst Island, while McClintock and his six companions made for Melville Island. The last stage of the march proved to be particularly exhausting as the sea pressure had forced the ice into 20-foot-high hummocks – a considerable obstacle as they approached the island. Passing by Cape Dundas – Parry's most westerly point in 1819 – McClintock's party made its way to Bushnan Cove, where they found the wheels of Parry's cart, abandoned during an overland expedition in 1820. At the site of Parry's winter harbour, relics of his expedition were found, the most impressive of which was a large sandstone block upon which Surgeon Fisher had carved an inscription in 1820. Of Franklin and his men they found no trace.

> On 1st June I reached Bushnan Cove and, taking four men with me, entered the ravine at its head; spreading ourselves across, we walked up it and soon found the encampment of Sir Edward Parry when here on 11th June 1820. The very accurate account published by him at once guided me to his record, his ammunition and the remains of his broken cart. The crevices between the stones piled over the record were filled with ice and its tin case had been eaten through with rust. The powder had been destroyed by wet. We erected a cairn on the spot and placed within it a record, then gathering a few relics of our pred-ecessors, we returned with the remains of the cart to our encampment; an excellent fire had been made with willow-stems, which soon thawed the ice out of Parry's record tin; the record was carefully removed but little more than the date was distinguishable. Had it been in a better state of preservation, I would have restored it to its lonely position.[38]

Disappointed at their failure to unravel the mystery of Franklin, McClintock and his men began their home-ward march on 6 June 1851.

Throughout the expedition McClintock had taken great care with the men's health, checking their feet and faces for frostbite. Snow-blindness was a great danger, and he insisted that the men take eye drops every day in an effort to keep it at bay. But just as they neared the end of their long journey, some of the men developed ailments. He later wrote:

> My medical skill was put to the test here and found wanting: John Salmon complained of violent pain in his chest and difficulty in breathing. It was agreed by the men that this complaint was 'wind in the stomach' and they recommended peppermint drops. I was provided with medicines and instructions for their uses, well adapted to ordinary occasions but this complaint was not in my Medical Dictionary, neither were the peppermint drops in my Materia Medica. Supposing that something he had eaten disagreed with him, I acceded to the proposal of the party and ordered half a gallon of warm salt water to be administered, which, acting as an emetic, afforded some relief. At this time we were subsisting upon musk-ox beef, which we consumed in enormous quantities, with a little biscuit only, not having even pepper and salt; subsequently, when we had plenty of both, Salmon had a second attack; but this time he did not call in my aid; he told me he cured himself in half an hour, by swallowing a large draught of pepper and salt.[39]

The return journey was more gruelling than the outward trip due to a partial thaw caused by an increase in temperature. Trudging through partially melted ice and snow, the extreme cold gave way to conditions that left the men constantly soaked. McClintock wrote:

Musk ox: this stuffed specimen, brought back by McClintock, is now displayed in Dublin's Natural History Museum.

June 21st. For the last three hours our journey was very fatiguing, as we had to cross pools of water, crusted over with a mixture of ice and recently fallen snow, an inch and a half thick, yet not strong enough to bear. The men had to break the ice before the sledge, which cut their boots and hurt their feet.

June 23rd. Started under sail, a pleasant breeze blowing. Three hours of very severe labour were spent in reaching the Point – a distance of two miles. A great part of this time was spent in digging the sledge out of the deep, soft, clogging snow. Occasionally we had to unload the sledge and carry everything forward to better ice.[40]

When, on 4 July, *Assistance* was reached, McClintock

and his men had been away from the ship for exactly 80 days, and had travelled just over 770 miles.[41] The other parties had also covered impressive distances. Bradford had examined 100 miles of coastline on the east side of Melville Island, Captain Ommanney, Sherard Osborn and Willy Browne had searched in the direction of Cape Walker, while Captain Penny had searched the Wellington Channel. In all, they had covered 7,025 miles, surveying 1,225 miles of unknown coastline.

On 11 August 1851 the ships left their winter quarters, searching Jones Sound on their return journey. On reaching England, the crew of the *Assistance* were paid off at Woolwich. It was October 1851 and, as he went on yet another well-earned leave to Ireland, McClintock had to accept that, while he had carried out important survey work during his long-range sledging expedition, he had failed in his ultimate goal. One other unpalatable truth had to be faced up to: a large and well-organised expedition had gone to the Arctic in search of Franklin and had discovered absolutely no trace of the expedition's whereabouts. Leopold McClintock was increasingly of the view that they were searching in the wrong area.

CHAPTER EIGHT

The Admiralty Perplexed

The lack of any concrete information as to the fate of the Franklin expedition was a profound disappointment for the general public. In London, Admiralty officials considered what to do. The Arctic Committee, made up of seven experienced polar explorers and three Admiralty officials, pondered the complete lack of evidence regarding Franklin's location. The committee had been established in the mid-1830s as an advisory group to future Arctic expeditions, but since the death of Sir John Barrow in November 1848 had lacked a certain energy and focus. Some committee members questioned the advisability of sending any further search expeditions, and some felt certain that Franklin's ships had sunk and that he and his crews had perished.

The public and, perhaps more importantly, Lady Franklin were having none of this. In 1851 she funded a private expedition that saw the *Prince Albert* sail to the Arctic under the command of Captain William Kennedy, assisted by the flamboyant Lieutenant Joseph-René Bellot. They explored Somerset Island and much of Boothia. In 1852 the indefatigable Lady Franklin sent Edward Inglefield in the *Isabel* to search north of Baffin Bay. Neither expedition found evidence of the missing ships and men.

In light of these failures the initiative returned to the Arctic Committee, which now considered where any further search parties should go. A major flaw in its contemplations was that it failed to grasp the implications of Franklin's original orders. It was assumed, on the basis of no real evidence, that he had sailed northwards through Wellington Channel, since his original instructions were to travel southwest from Melville Island. It seemed logical to assume that he had sailed into Peel Sound, the next opening from Prince Regent Inlet – a route that would have allowed him to travel southwest along the west coast of Boothia and from there to King William Island. Previous expeditions had looked into Peel Sound and found it totally blocked with ice. On this basis it was assumed that Franklin had chosen his second option and sailed through Wellington Channel.

But what if Peel Sound had not been frozen when Franklin reached it? The ice conditions in the Arctic could change drastically from year to year. Captain Frederick W. Beechey of the Arctic Committee concluded that Franklin had found Peel Sound ice-free and, following his original orders, had sailed southwest through the strait. Any search, he asserted, should be concentrated on the mouth of the Great Fish River and along adjacent coasts. Dr Richard King, an experienced overland explorer, proposed a similar course of action. He felt sure that evidence of Franklin would be found along the west coast of Boothia. Opinion on the Arctic Committee, however, was resolutely opposed to them. Yet Beechey and King would ultimately be proved correct.

There was also a failure to correctly grasp the implications of what had been found on Beechey Island – or rather, what had *not* been found. Though there was ample

The graves of John Torrington, John Hartnell
and William Braine.

evidence that Franklin's men had camped there, it was
standard practice to build a stone cairn and leave a record
of any developments and future plans within it. Yet none
was found on Beechey Island, and it was assumed that
Franklin had simply neglected to leave one. But it was just
as likely that he had not left one as he had no intention
of deviating from his original orders. He was heading to
Peel Sound. The significance of the three graves on Beechey
Island was also not understood. Why had three men died
so early in the expedition? The searchers, so relieved to
find only three graves, failed to recognise the indication
of a serious failure in the health of Franklin's crews.

The Arctic Committee displayed no sense of urgency
as it pondered where it should send ships. It announced
a series of rewards for information as to Franklin's whereabouts, and discussed various ludicrous theories for
rescue – some of which were later adopted, including

message collars attached to Arctic foxes.

McClintock remained on leave in Dublin, staying with his mother and sisters at 2 Gardiner Place. During this period, he experimented with various types of cooking equipment and fuels in the hope of perfecting his Arctic cooking methods. He also became prominent in the Dublin scientific community, and was befriended by Samuel Haughton (1821–97), an eminent geologist, engineer and scientist, and distinguished member of the Royal Irish Academy. Haughton recognised the importance of McClintock's geological and zoological discoveries, and encouraged him to share them with the world through a series of lectures and publications. Later, Haughton would deliver lectures on McClintock's Arctic expeditions at the Royal Irish Academy.

Early in 1852 the Arctic Committee announced the formation of another search expedition. It also let it be known that this was the last expedition the Admiralty intended to fund. McClintock was appointed as one of the expedition officers, which was to be commanded by Captain Sir Edward Belcher. It was to be one of the most disastrous and acrimonious polar expeditions ever.

CHAPTER NINE

To the Arctic with Belcher

For this latest – and final – Franklin search expedition, four vessels were commissioned: the *Assistance*, *Pioneer*, *Resolute* and *Intrepid*. On the advice of the Arctic Committee, two ships were to travel through Wellington Channel while the other two would explore the area around Melville Island – extending the area covered by McClintock in his previous searches. The *North Star*, under Captain Pullen, would later be assigned to the flotilla as a depot ship, with orders to harbour at Beechey Island.

Beside its brief to find Franklin, the expedition's officers had another concern – the whereabouts of McClure and the crew of *Investigator*. McClure had left Portsmouth in January 1850 in company with HMS *Enterprise*, under the command of Captain Richard Collinson. The two ships parted company in April during a gale in the North Pacific, and McClure had not been heard from since. The Admiralty appended the search for McClure to the mission to find the missing Franklin expedition.

The appointment of Sir Edward Belcher as expedition commander would prove to be a disastrous decision. Though an experienced explorer – having previously served as a surveyor on the *Blossom* during an Arctic

Captain Sir Edward Belcher (centre), with Captain Henry Kellett (left) and Captain W.J.S. Pullen.

expedition of 1825–28 – he was in poor health and, as became increasingly obvious, his nerve had failed.

In February 1852 McClintock was appointed to command the *Intrepid*, which was to act as tender to the *Resolute*, commanded by Henry Kellett. This was his first command and, while the whole expedition was under Belcher's orders, *Resolute* and *Intrepid* formed a separate division which, on reaching the Arctic, would operate independently. The Tipperary-born Kellett was known for his ability and good nature, and he and McClintock would get on well.

During the spring of 1852 the preparations for the new expedition got underway. The *Intrepid* had damaged her false keel in August 1851 during her most recent expedition to the Arctic. The fitting of a new keel and the enlargement of the officers' wardroom was supervised by McClintock, who also had a number of stoves fitted so as to heat all areas of the ship during the Arctic winter. His final preparation was to ensure that *Intrepid* had a good library, as an ample supply of reading material would be of prime importance during the winter months.

On 15 April 1852 the squadron of ships left Woolwich. After a stormy Atlantic crossing, the Whale Fish Islands were reached on 29 May. The voyage through Melville Bay proved particularly difficult that summer, prompting a number of whaling ships to accompany the expedition's ships in the hope of an easier passage. Two were crushed, their wooden hulls imploding under the pressure of ice, and only one whaler succeeded in reaching the 'North Water' alongside the expedition's ships.

McClintock was kept extremely busy aboard *Intrepid*, pulling the other ships free from the ice. On 24 June the *Resolute* was severely nipped by the ice and, listing at 30 degrees, was only pulled clear with some difficulty. At other times the whole flotilla could not find a lead through the ice, and leads had to be opened by engaging in sawing operations and blasting with gunpowder. Ice docks were also cut out to provide temporary shelter.

By 1 August 1852 *Intrepid* had towed the *Resolute*, the *North Star* and a whaler into the 'North Water'. By 10 August they had reached Beechey Island, where Captain Pullen thankfully installed the *North Star* as depot ship. McClintock went back in search of *Assistance*, the expedition's ships having become separated in dense fog. Having located her he towed her to Beechey Island before taking *Intrepid* as far as Cape Bowden. On his return he reported that Wellington Channel was free of ice.

During his last Arctic expedition with Captain Austin, McClintock had been anxious to land at Beechey Island but had no opportunity to do so. He now examined the remains of Franklin's first winter quarters and explored the island. On 15 August Belcher led *Assistance* and *Pioneer* through Wellington Channel, and two days later entered a winter harbour. The two divisions of the expedition now went their separate ways, with Kellett and McClintock proceeding westwards towards Melville Island. This island had first been reached by Parry during his 1819–20 expedition, and though McClintock had sledged there during his previous expedition, no other ships had ever visited the island.

Navigation presented considerable problems, and Kellett and McClintock had to constantly make adjustments for magnetic variation. Sea conditions were extremely dangerous – on one occasion *Resolute* was grounded off Cornwallis Island and pressed by a heavy ice floe. They briefly found good sailing conditions off Griffith Island, but found themselves facing an ice-bound sea again off Lowther Island, which they explored. When open water was finally reached – off Bathurst Island – they encountered very rough seas. To the south were large fields of pack ice, but the ships continued to press westwards, passing between ice fields and land.

On 1 September 1852 McClintock and Kellett arrived at Melville Island – it was the thirty-third anniversary of Parry's discovery of the island in 1819. Having decided to over-winter at Bridport Inlet, shooting parties were immediately sent out to secure fresh meat for the crews.

McClintock now wanted to make best use of what remained of the 'fine' weather and was determined to establish supply depots away from the ships before the onset of winter. Four days after arriving at Melville Island, McClintock – accompanied by Dr Scott and thirteen men – set out on an overland journey, this time using two small carts, as he would be travelling on land rather than ice. He later admitted this was a terrible idea. Even before he reached the shore, the carts broke through the ice and sank into the water, damaging some provisions. The stores were replaced and the party set out again, heading towards the interior of Melville Island. The carts proved to be totally unsuitable in the soft snow and frequently had to be dug out. Once more, the expedition returned to the ship. Three days later it set out again, this time with sledges. But soon after leaving, Petty Officer George Drover collapsed and had to return to the ship, his place being taken by one of the ship's engineers, Thomas R. Purchase. It is interesting to note that Wilkie, Salmon and Hood had served with McClintock before and were with him again on this trip.

For this journey the party was away for 40 days. Several other parties had also left the ship, preparing depots for the following year's sledging operations. McClintock later wrote of his efforts to establish a depot:

> Having secured our ships near Dealy Island, Bridport Inlet, early in September, we commenced preparations for carrying out depots of provisions, in furtherance of our intended spring explorations, as soon as enough of snow should have fallen to enable our sledges to travel. But as I was to cross Melville Island to the north, I set out at once, with two light, strong carts, each drawn by eight men and heavily laden. Our first mishap was breaking through the ice, whereby considerable loss of provisions and delay were occasioned. My good rifle sank to rise no more. We succeeded in depositing our depot at Point Nias (about fifty miles only from our ships), after six weeks of intense labour; half this time we

worked with carts, and then when snow had fallen, we used sledges. The interior of the country we gained by ascending a ravine; we then traversed a stony, barren plain, intersected by numerous deep ravines with precipitous sides. The general level of this central plateau was about 600 feet above the sea. For the first eighteen days we did not see a living creature. After the middle of October we saw several reindeer migrating westward, where we subsequently discovered their favourite feeding grounds. When travelling through the ravines our progress was occasionally almost prevented by the ice-cliffs, or glaciers, attached to their sides and protruding nearly across.[42]

Commenting on the severe conditions he wrote:

Here we were weather-bound by a gale for a day. Temperature at zero, and in the tent at +10. The men agreed in voting noses to be a nuisance in this country, especially prominent ones, as they are usually the first part frost-bitten. Whiskers and moustaches were also condemned, not only as being useless, but most inconvenient – the former catching all the snowdrift, and one's breath condensing on the latter, forms an icicle not easily removed.[43]

He described the back-breaking toil involved in travelling over such terrain:

It would occupy too much space even to

enumerate the difficulties of this cart journey;
the carts were ill-adapted, the diameter of the
wheels being only three feet; they frequently
stuck fast in the snow, and had to be dug out,
carried forward and reloaded. Sometimes we
had to lower them over very steep banks; at
others to advance by standing pulls with the
drag-ropes shifted to the upper rims of the
wheels; when this expedient failed, we had to
'dig out'. The men were ready at expedients,
no matter what the difficulty was, and their
perseverance and ingenuity entitled them to
great praise. In crossing rocky ground, when
one wheel or the other was almost constantly
brought up, the man whose duty it was to
guide the cart by the pole in front, was tossed
about from side to side like a shuttlecock; he
had to cling to it to prevent being knocked
over, and to exert great patience, skill, and
temper; in going down hill it was a post of real
danger. In every difficulty we found our nauti-
cal education a most valuable acquisition; and
for downright hard tugging, no men could
have endured such fatigue, unless, like
seamen, they had been inured from boyhood
to dragging at ropes.[44]

McClintock and his party returned to *Intrepid* on 25
October 'in perfect health and with half a day's provisions
remaining'.

The sledging operations at an end, McClintock busied
himself in preparing for the onset of winter. He ensured
his provisions were sufficient and well stored, and made
sure his crew had adequate winter clothing. In an effort

to forestall boredom during the winter months, he established instructional classes. Aboard *Intrepid* he established the *Soirée Fantastique*, which consisted of conjuring acts, comic songs and a farce entitled *Pat and the Magistrate*. Similar entertainments took place aboard *Resolute* under the supervision of Lieutenant George F. Mecham. The ships' officers and men visited each other for dinner, and Christmas and New Year's Eve were occasions for great celebration.

The one dark cloud over these festivities was the death of George Drover, who passed away on 12 December 1852. His health had failed to recover since his earlier collapse, and he had slowly failed. With great difficulty, a grave was hacked out of the ice, and he was buried on 19 December, McClintock conducting the funeral service.

Throughout winter McClintock prepared for the following season's sledging, and came up with the idea of 'satellite sledges', whereby smaller parties of two to three men using small sledges would be dispatched from the main party to hunt or explore coastal inlets. It was his intention to explore as far to the northwest as was possible, while Mecham would explore to the west, and Lieutenant Richard Vesey Hamilton would travel due north. Ensign Emile de Bray – a French officer seconded to the expedition – was to act as McClintock's depot officer, and in early 1853 they went on a series of training marches together.

When the final preparations had been made, McClintock's team of eight men would have to pull two sledges, each weighing around 1,000 pounds. Wilkie and Hood had both taken ill and would not accompany him; only John Salmon remained from his original sledge party. By April 1853 all was ready for yet another epic sledging expedition.

To Melville Island and Beyond

As became the tradition in polar travel, the sledges for this expedition were given names and mottoes, and supplied with flags. McClintock's sledge was christened *Star of the North*, its motto 'Be Thou Our Guide'. He planned to travel even further north on this occasion, and intended to cross Melville Island. Indeed, all the sledge parties would travel to Melville Island before branching off to search in different directions.

The initial going was extremely tough as they ploughed through soft snow in gale-force conditions. A partial thaw left footwear, clothing and bedding sodden, and these items could only be dried with difficulty. From Point Nias, one of the support parties headed back to the ships, while another, under Mate Richard Roche, headed northeast to establish a depot.[45]

McClintock, accompanied by a support sledge commanded by the French officer, de Bray, continued along the northern coast of Melville Island as far as Cape Fisher, which was reached on 19 April 1853. Cape Fisher represented the limit of Parry's explorations in 1820 – the area beyond this point had never been explored. McClintock later described the initial phase of this expedition:

On the 4th of April 1853, seventy-seven out of
the eighty-eight individuals composing the
crews of the *Resolute* and *Intrepid* renewed the
sledge-search for our missing countrymen.
This time I was accompanied by Monsieur
Emile de Bray, Enseigne de Vaisseau, in the
French navy, who came in command of a
supply sledge. This officer had been attached
to the expedition in order to obtain a knowledge of Arctic exploration. We crossed the
land as before, nothing of interest happening,
except four and a half days' detention by a
most violent north-wester, the temperature
varying from 10 to 30 below zero. In our tent
it was generally several degrees below zero. At
Point Nias we completed provisions to fifty-
three days, and after passing Cape Fisher, the
extreme point seen by Parry in 1820, our
discoveries commenced. Oxen and reindeer
were seen here. Following the tread of the
coast-line to the north west, we reached cape
Scott, in 76° North and 115° W.; from thence
it inclined to the south-west to Cape Russell.
Having completed this N.W. side of Melville
Island, Monsieur de Bray left with me all the
provisions he could spare, and returned to the
ship. I then proceeded to explore the off-lying
land, now known as Prince Patrick Island.[46]

During a day spent repairing damage to the sledges,
three musk oxen appeared. McClintock managed to shoot
one, which provided the party with a welcome supply of
fresh meat so early in the journey. But the going became
increasingly tough. The ice over which they travelled was

old and rough, while the snow was deep, soft and wet, as it thawed in the improving spring conditions. In some respects, travelling in the 'improving' weather presented more problems than sledging in the extreme cold of winter, when the ground was a solid – and dry – mass of ice and snow.

When McClintock's party reached the north-west point of Melville Island, it turned south with a view to examining the west coast. Mecham was exploring to the west, and in this way the two parties would be able to examine the entire west coast of Melville Island and search for traces of Franklin and his men.

En route they surveyed large areas of new coastline, giving names to various promontories and inlets – one was named Cape de Bray in honour of the leader of McClintock's support party. McClintock would later learn of de Bray's eventful return journey to the ships. He had been accompanied by Hood and two other men whose health had broken down, and near Point Nias a stoker named John Coombs fell down dead from exhaustion. By the time de Bray and his men returned to the ships on 17 May they had been absent for 45 days and had travelled over 380 miles.

Meanwhile, as McClintock continued southwards along the western coast of Melville Island, he put into action his newly devised system of utilising satellite sledges. Taking a small sledge and two men – Giddy and Drew – he detached himself from the main party and headed southwards. Equipped and supplied with nothing more than sleeping bags and four days' provisions, this was an extremely risky undertaking. The three men continued south until they reached a large bay, which McClintock christened Cape Purchase in honour of Thomas Purchase, an engineer aboard *Resolute*.

McClintock, Giddy and Drew rejoined the main party on 8 May. McClintock now decided to travel even further west, as a large body of unknown land was visible in that direction. The strait between Melville Island and this unknown land was crossed, and on 14 May McClintock and his crew became the first white men to set foot upon it, though McClintock did not know this at the time. He would later christen it Prince Patrick Island, and call the point at which they landed Cape Wilkie, in honour of his old shipmate.

McClintock and his crew set out to explore this land in the hope of finding traces of the Franklin expedition. The terrain was equally difficult on Prince Patrick Island, the ground being covered in deep, soft snow. He later wrote:

> This traverse was more difficult from the great
> load upon our sledge, and the unfavourable
> state of the ice and snow. The freshly fallen
> snow was soft and deep, and beneath it the
> older snow lay in furrows across our route,
> hardened and polished by winter gales and
> drifts, so that it resembled marble.[47]

The men marched northwest along the coast of a deep inlet that they named Intrepid Inlet. The main party under McClintock and a satellite party under Green explored this new area thoroughly. McClintock continued northwards and, while crossing another strait, discovered and named the Polnia Islands, one of which he christened Ireland's Eye, no doubt a reference to the small island of the same name off the coast of Dublin.

The most northerly point reached was 77° 43' north. During the course of the next few weeks the coast of Prince Patrick Island was scoured for some sign of

Franklin having passed that way. Many geographical features were given names, such as Cape Giddy, Salmon Point and Green Bay – all names connected with members of the sledge crews. On the north coast of Prince Patrick Island, a point was christened Cape McClintock.

During this journey the sledge crews became increasingly demoralised. The improvement in the weather had led to a mild thaw which made travelling extremely uncomfortable. The thawing snow left clothes, footwear and bedding dripping wet. On several occasions the men had to battle through gale-force winds. McClintock wrote of being caught in one of these gales:

> On the 22nd [May] it blew a violent gale, and the temperature fell to -14. After the recent warm weather, we felt this searching blast as if it was blowing through our frames as freely as it did through the holes in our garments. In the midst of this I rejoined my party, who were snugly encamped at the appointed rendezvous. I never fully appreciated the shelter of a tent until then.[48]

The misery of these conditions is illustrated by the unofficial name McClintock's men gave to a place on Prince Patrick Island – 'Torture Cove'.

On 25 June the satellite parties regrouped at Cape Giddy and McClintock took a decision to explore a small island lying in the northern part of the channel between Melville Island and Prince Patrick Island. The island was reached on 27 June and, in memory of his old homeland, McClintock christened it Emerald Island. He later wrote:

> The flattering title of 'Emerald Island' was

conferred upon the island we next visited, rather in the comparative than the positive meaning of the word. It certainly has much moss, and altogether a better show of green than the contiguous shores of Prince Patrick's and Melville Islands; yet its surface appeared very like a ploughed field after an unusual deluge of rain – a dark, rich, tenacious clay, more laborious to walk upon than the sludge-encumbered floe. The centre of the island rises to about 250 feet above the sea, with gradual slopes and low shores.[49]

On 29 June the sledge teams turned south and headed back to the safety of the ships at Bridport Inlet on Melville Island. McClintock realised, perhaps too late, that the men had reached the limit of their endurance. In the difficult summer conditions, they were becoming increasingly exhausted, as McClintock noted in his journal:

4th July. Midnight, halted to lunch. These halts are always disagreeable. At the commencement of our journey we were obliged to keep moving about to prevent our feet being frost-bitten, whilst we got through a few mouthfuls of frozen bacon as dextrously as we could, with huge mitts on. At this season we have also to keep moving about, to prevent our feet getting benumbed, which they are always too ready to do after walking several hours through the ice-cold water; and just now our upper garments, which have escaped the splashing, are saturated by four hours' rain. Under all circumstances we have one unfailing comfort, in the welcome drop of grog, which constitutes the only enjoyable part of our nightly luncheons.[50]

During the trek back to the ships, relics of Parry's 1820 expedition were discovered at Point Nias. McClintock later wrote of the discovery:

> Arrived at Point Nias. I proceeded to examine Parry's monument, and copied the record left by him when here in June 1820. After carefully replacing it, together with my own, and a small chart of recent discoveries, I commenced a search for the site of his encampment. I fortunately found it close to the beach, and very near my own. We recognised it by the stones arranged for keeping down the sides of his tent: a few large ones were placed within, as if they had served for seats or pillows. I picked up several pieces of white line, rope-yarn and wood, whilst so engaged the men made a still further and more startling discovery – the narrow rimmed wheels of Sir E. Parry's cart had left *tracks*, still wonderfully distinct, in the soft, wet earth, thinly coated with moss!! In one place these cart-tracks were continuous for thirty yards, and they were also very distinct where the cart, having come from the eastward, turned up towards the encampment. No lichens had grown upon the upturned stones, and even their deep beds in the soil, whence Parry's men removed them, were generally distinct. In two or three cases we recognised at a glance the stone to which each had belonged. This astonishing

freshness of traces, after a lapse of thirty-three
years, compels us to assign a very considerable antiquity to the circles of stones and
other Esquimaux traces which we find spar-
ingly strewed along the southern shores of the
Parry group, since they are always moss-
covered, and often indistinct.[51]

By the time they reached Point Nias – on 12 July –
Hiccles was seriously ill. McClintock administered first
aid and Hiccles was strapped to a sledge. But the terrain
was extremely difficult, and the men were suffering from
ill health while being obliged to drag one of their shipmates. McClintock now made a crucial decision. All
spare equipment, clothing, bedding and provisions were
abandoned. Each man was lightly equipped and carried
only emergency rations in a knapsack, and followed
McClintock in a dash southwards. They reached the ships
on 18 July.

In total, they had been away from the ships for 105
days and had travelled – when the satellite expeditions
are included – 1,210 miles. McClintock's party had
surveyed 768 miles of new coastline, and the other sledge
parties had also done well. Mecham had travelled to the
west, had discovered Eglinton Island, and had made it to
the south-east point of Prince Patrick Island. His party
had christened Cape Mecham and Cape Manning, and
had explored the area not visited by McClintock, thus
completing the survey of Prince Patrick Island. Mecham's
party had travelled just over 1,000 miles in 91 days,
surveying 785 miles of undiscovered coastline. The party
led by Vesey Hamilton had explored the northern coast
of Melville Island, discovering Murchison Island. His party
was away for 54 days, travelling 568 miles.[52]

Each of these expeditions was a minor triumph of Arctic exploration and endurance. Collectively, they had increased the geographical knowledge of the region and filled in many of the 'blank' spaces on the Admiralty's charts. McClintock later summed up the expeditions as follows:

> Truly may we, Arctic explorers, exclaim 'Knowledge is Power!' It is now a comparatively easy matter to start with six or eight men, and a sledge laden with six or seven weeks' provisions, and to travel some 600 miles across desert wastes and frozen seas, from which no sustenance can be obtained. There is now no known position, however remote, that a well-equipped crew could not effect their escape from by their own unaided efforts. We felt this; and by our experience gained in a cause more glorious than ever men embarked in, have secured all future Arctic explorers a plan by which they may rejoin their fellow men. I will not venture to define the exact ration in which risk of life has thus been diminished; but I can confidently affirm that, had Franklin and Crozier's crews this experience to guide them, they would undoubtedly have abandoned their ice-bound ships and, in all human probability, would have been long ago restored to their native land.[53]

Robert McClure.

CHAPTER ELEVEN

Belcher's Failure

When McClintock returned to the ships, he found they had been joined by the crew of McClure's *Investigator*. McClure was alive, but his crew was in a dreadful state. During the course of his expedition, he had rounded the north-west point of America and discovered a channel he christened the Prince of Wales Strait. By September 1850, however, his vessel had become beset in the ice. Exploring parties were sent out on foot and, by October 1850, McClure had ascertained that the Prince of Wales Strait opened into Melville Sound. Incredibly, he had discovered a Northwest Passage.

Though the ice eventually relinquished its hold on *Investigator*, the ship enjoyed only a temporary reprieve, and by September 1851 was again trapped by ice, this time in the misnamed Bay of Mercy. Here it would remain.

During the autumn of 1852 Lieutenant George F. Mecham had discovered a record left by McClure at Winter Harbour. Dated April 1851, it told of the *Investigator*'s previous movements and its current position, beset in Bay of Mercy. During the preceding years, McClure had pushed southeast through the Arctic, undertaking some notable sledge journeys. In the summer of

1851 he moved the *Investigator* to Bay of Mercy on the north coast of Banks Island, where the ship became beset in the ice. During the spring of 1852 he went on more sledge journeys, leaving the record that Mecham had found at Winter Harbour on Melville Island. In the meantime, the men still aboard *Investigator* endured a nightmare existence as their rations slowly dwindled. Securely beset in the ice, morale plummeted as the men feared they would all die in the ice trap of Bay of Mercy.

When he discovered the location of *Investigator*, Kellett sent Lieutenant Bedford Pim to communicate with McClure. Pim and his sledge team travelled over 200 miles in order to reach *Investigator* – on 6 April 1853 – and on arrival, Pim was dismayed at the pitiable condition of the crew. Yet despite the fact that his men were obviously incapable of any further effort, McClure was still intent on completing a Northwest Passage – the Admiralty prize of £10,000, not to mention the instant fame that the feat would bring, had severely clouded his judgement.

When the sick members of *Investigator*'s crew reached Kellett's ships in April, Kellett immediately countermanded McClure's orders, and directed him to abandon ship and to bring his men aboard the *Intrepid* and *Resolute*. A medical examination confirmed the poor state of McClure's crew – most had scurvy and others were frost-bitten, while some had gone mad. On 17 June 1853 McClure brought the last of his crew to the ships.

McClure's actions as commander of the *Investigator* continue to be debated by polar historians. Without doubt, he had subjected his men to a dreadful ordeal, and had persisted in his attempt on the Northwest Passage when all hope of completing one unaided had been lost. Yet he *had* completed a Northwest Passage of sorts – he was the first man to travel from the Pacific to the Atlantic

HMS Investigator *beset in ice off the north coast of Baring Island, 20 August 1851.*

via the Arctic, though in doing so, he had travelled by ship, sledge and on foot. Following much debate, the Admiralty would later award him the £10,000 prize money.

McClintock returned from his sledge journey to find the numbers aboard *Intrepid* and *Resolute* swelled by the ailing remnants of McClure's crew. In mid-August 1853 the ice broke up and the two ships drifted out of Bridport Inlet. But the summer of 1853 saw a sudden deterioration in the weather. The ships were stopped by ice near Point Griffiths, off the south-east coast of Melville Island. By 22 August they were beset once again in the ice, having made but little progress to the east. Soon, even the drifting of the ice ceased, and they came to a total halt 26 miles southwest of Cape Cockburn on Bathurst Island. It was now obvious that they faced yet another winter in the Arctic.

For McClintock, Kellett and their crews, it would be

their second winter. They were still in good health and well provisioned, and the prospect was not too daunting. For the unfortunate members of McClure's crew, this would be their fourth winter. It must have seemed their nightmare would never end. Yet even the crews of *Intrepid* and *Resolute* were beginning to fall sick. During the winter of 1853–54, McClintock's old shipmates, Hood and Wilkie, fell ill and died.

In an effort to maintain morale, a programme of winter activities was organised. The unpopular 'school lessons' were dropped in favour of a series of entertainments. Frederick Krabbe, master of the *Resolute*, put on conjuring shows, and several farces and plays – including *The Taming of the Shrew* – were staged.

In the spring of 1854 it was decided to re-establish contact with Sir Edward Belcher. Vesey Hamilton started out by sledge in March, and found Belcher and his ships beset in Wellington Channel, 52 miles north of Beechey Island. The scene that met Hamilton was not good. Belcher had always been known for his irascibility, but allowances had previously been made because of his competence as an officer. During the winter of 1853–54 – when the ships under his command became beset in the ice – he lost his nerve, and became terrified of being nipped in the ice. As he ferried himself from *Pioneer* to *Assistance* and back again, he became an almost comical sight. Worse, he had become paranoid, suspecting that his officers were plotting against him. As in an Arctic version of the *Caine Mutiny*, Belcher had his officers put under arrest, threatening courts martial in London on their return. By the time Hamilton reached him, Belcher was convinced that the ships of the expedition would be crushed and should be abandoned, and that the crews should try to run for home aboard the depot ship, the *North Star*.

Hamilton returned to the *Resolute* carrying Belcher's orders, contained in a long, rambling and often contradictory document. Having given Belcher's order due consideration, McClintock and Kellett drafted a letter to Belcher in which they stated that their position did not require them to abandon ship. They were well provisioned, safely positioned and, furthermore, their original orders did not cover the possibility of abandoning the two ships. Both Kellett and McClintock were sure they could continue to the east in the navigable season of 1854.

It was decided that McClintock would travel to Belcher himself to outline the foolishness of his orders. On 13 April, he set out for the *Assistance*. On this occasion, he travelled with a dog-team, and was amazed at their speed and efficiency. He reached the *North Star* on 18 April, and set out next morning in the direction of *Assistance*, covering 52 miles in just 24 hours. It was yet another opportunity for him to test his ideas on Arctic travel, and he would later experiment further in the use of dog-teams, although he would never lose his preference for man-hauling sledges.

On reaching *Assistance*, McClintock spent the next 24 hours trying to talk Belcher out of his proposed course of action. It was in vain – *Intrepid*, *Resolute*, *Pioneer* and *Assistance* were to be abandoned, while the crews would crowd aboard the *North Star* and head for England. Now that Belcher had issued a direct order for McClintock and Kellett to abandon their ships, McClintock headed back, arriving on 28 May. He had sledged over 460 miles in fifteen days.

Both McClintock and Kellett were determined to leave their ships in as best a condition as possible. They were cleaned, hatches battened down and their remaining provisions stored away. Messages were sent out to sledging parties under Mecham and Krabbe, telling them to go directly to Beechey Island.

On 15 June, the crews of *Intrepid* and *Resolute* commenced their dismal journey to the *North Star*, reaching it on 28 June. The various ships' crews now crowded aboard the *North Star,* and made ready for an uncomfortable and dangerous journey home.

On 17 July, Belcher arrived from *Assistance*, sitting in a boat on a sledge dragged by ten men, oblivious to the hardships of his crew. Now installed aboard the *North Star*, the weight of argument brought upon him by the various officers caused him to briefly change his mind. McClintock suggested that a volunteer crew should return to *Assistance* in the hope of extracting it when the ice broke up. Volunteers duly stepped forward, and Belcher remounted his Arctic charabanc and allowed them to drag him back over the ice to the *Assistance*. After a torturous journey, they arrived on 23 August. But Belcher was still fearful, and the next morning – having changed his mind – he repeated the order to abandon ship. McClintock's entreaties were in vain, and he and his men were left with the humiliating task of dragging their fearful – and possibly insane – commander back to the *North Star*.

Thankfully, two other transport ships – the *Phoenix* and the *Talbot* – had arrived, and the homeless crews were dispersed among these ships. In October 1854 the last Admiralty-sponsored search expedition returned to England. It was an ignominious failure. A series of courts martial saw McClintock and his brother officers exonerated, having been ordered by Belcher to abandon their ships. Belcher was also acquitted, due to the discretion the Admiralty had allowed him in his orders. Yet in the court, his sword was handed back to him in stony silence. He would never again command a ship.[54]

CHAPTER TWELVE

Half-pay Captain

On his return from the Arctic McClintock was promoted to captain. Yet it was an extremely depressing time for him. His mother had died in January 1854, and his homecoming to Dublin was tinged with an incredible sadness. In addition he had been associated with the greatest failure in the history of Arctic exploration. Despite the Admiralty having cleared him of all blame, he must have wondered if the Belcher disaster would damage his future career prospects. The Crimean War had broken out in March 1854, yet he had not been sent on active service. The Royal Navy was fully engaged in the Black Sea, while its ships were also blockading Russian ports in the Baltic and the Pacific. Thousands of sailors – including many of his own countrymen – were serving with the Naval Brigade in the trenches before Sevastopol, but McClintock remained unemployed, eking out an existence as a half-pay captain in Dublin.

The Admiralty now confirmed it had no intention of dispatching further Franklin search expeditions. Franklin's name, and those of his officers, had been discreetly removed from the *Navy List* earlier in the year at the very moment the first real news concerning their fates emerged. In July 1854 a report from Dr John Rae of the Hudson's Bay Company detailed his discoveries during an expedition to the west coast of Boothia. Rae met Inuit in Pelly Bay who told of having seen a party of around 40 white men dragging a boat. According to the Inuit these men had died of hunger, with 30 of their bodies being discovered on an island near the mouth of a large river, and 5 more nearby. Rae believed this to be Montreal Island, at the mouth of the Great Fish River. He purchased several items from the Inuit that were later confirmed as having belonged to Franklin and his men, including Franklin's medal of the Hanoverian Order, and pieces of silver plate stamped with the initials and crests of Franklin, Crozier and other officers of the expedition.

Later, James A. Anderson of the Hudson's Bay Company travelled to Montreal Island, and found the remains of a boat and scattered debris, among them tools and cooking utensils. Despite several representations to the Admiralty calling on it to search for the remains of Franklin and his men, it was satisfied with the information to hand. Franklin and his men were dead.

It would be left to Lady Franklin to organise a new search expedition. She was supported by members of the scientific community who, in June 1856, sent a petition to Lord Palmerston, the prime minister. Support also came from members of the peerage, the legal profession and innumerable naval and army officers. Finally, Lady Franklin lobbied Lord Palmerston personally. To give him his due, Palmerston was not entirely unsympathetic. But Sir Charles Wood, first lord of the Admiralty, and Sir Maurice Berkeley, the first sea lord, were adamant: the Admiralty would send no more ships in search of Franklin.

Having organised a previous search expedition – four years earlier, when she had sent Captain Edward Inglefield to search aboard *Isabel* – Lady Franklin resigned herself to having to do so again, financing the venture from her own funds together with monies raised from family, friends and members of the scientific and business communities. When she had secured sufficient funds, the *Fox* was purchased – a screw-propeller yacht of just 177-tons displacement.

In the meantime, though a massive naval building programme was underway, and despite hundreds of gun boats and 'floating batteries' being commissioned in what came to be known as the Great Armament, Leopold McClintock remained unemployed.

He took some small consolation in the fact that he was now a recognised authority on Arctic travel, and on the flora and fauna of the region. He had provided Sherard Osborn with material on the fauna of Perry Island when the latter was writing *Stray leaves from an Arctic journal* (London, 1852). In Dublin, McClintock addressed the Royal Dublin Society in January and May of 1856, talking on the subject of Arctic travel, and these lectures were later published in the society's journal.

McClintock had also emerged as a major figure in Lady Franklin's campaign to have another expedition sent in search of her husband. Writing to Sophia Cracroft from 48 Hardwicke Street in Dublin, he commented on the negative reaction of some in the Admiralty, pointing out how the Belcher disaster was influencing their opinion.

> I think Sir C. Wood's objections are very absurd. No one need expect much 'science and humanity' from one who has been so long a Lord of the Admiralty; but he knew well that the ships of the third expedition were abandoned not of necessity but by Admiralty order. As to the risk of being ice-bound, it is not necessary to incur

it. The danger of being crushed, a committee
of whaling captains would quickly dispose of,
and in the probable event of a detention, either
by being ice-bound or crushed, travellers will
say that there is no position so remote that they
could not effect their escape from it with
sledges and boats.[55]

McClintock had made a point of remaining in
constant contact with Lady Franklin, telling her of his
efforts among Dublin's scientific community to gain
support for a new search.

I have written to tell Dr Barker that Dr Robinson had been applied to, to stir up the Royal
Irish Academy and to hope that they would get
up a strong address.
P.S. I sincerely hope that Irishmen will be able
to 'pull together' for the men.[56]

When concluding a lecture, he stated:

It is in our power to rescue the survivors, or,
at least, to ascertain their fate, without peril-
ing a single life, and at a comparatively trifling
expense. That we refuse to do so is a deep
national disgrace.[57]

During this period in Dublin, he gave much thought
to the proposed expedition, and his letters make it obvious
that he hoped considerable resources would be made available. In a letter of early March 1857 he wrote to Lady
Franklin outlining his proposed course of action if he had
the use of the *Resolute* or the *Phoenix*, both steamers

of respectable size. Ultimately, she offered him a much more modest command. On 18 April 1857 Lady Franklin wrote to McClintock to request he take command of the *Fox*. He accepted the offer with alacrity, dispatching a reply from Dublin the same day:

> I have long-since thought the matter over and have, therefore, no hesitation in replying at once. The honourable post you offer me, I need not tell you, is most congenial to my feelings, and I at once accept it.[58]

With a remarkable candour for someone addressing the redoubtable Lady Franklin, he continued:

> I only accept the command for the eastern route and for the present year. I shall not risk detention of the *Fox* beyond one year, on any account, and therefore cannot winter between Bellot Strait and Gateshead Island but I may succeed in pushing through the unknown area, beyond the latter position. I can hardly reconcile myself to this great outlay and feel that it may be thought (by those who neither know you nor I) that I have helped or countenanced the sacrifices. Therefore I have been very silent and it is only when I see you cannot be diverted from your object, and in the belief that I am better able perhaps than most persons who may aspire to it, to conduct it to a successful issue, that I now, at the eleventh hour, accept the appointment I have so ardently desired. I shall always think that you are doing too much and think that having

set it on foot you ought to receive all the
subscriptions which may be offered.[59]

A week later, he travelled to London to begin preparations. Lord Wrottesley of the Royal Society and Sir Roder-
ick Murchison of the Royal Geographical Society assured
him of their support, as did Sir James Clark Ross, Captain
Austin and many other naval officers.

He was granted eighteen months leave by the Admiralty, which was generous considering that it still refused
to give him an active command. The Admiralty was not
so generous, however, when it came to releasing other
officers for the expedition. McClintock tried to secure
the services of Lieutenants Bob Aldrich, Bedford Pim and
George S. Nares, and Midshipman Henry Grey, all of whom
had previous Arctic experience. Grey, he wrote, had vast
experience of 'magnetic and surveying observations'.
Despite several pleading letters from McClintock, the
Admiralty refused to release them. McClintock also
requested the services of Bosun James Tullett and Thomas
Purchase, both of whom were old Arctic hands, but again
they were not released for the expedition. His old shipmate, John Salmon, requested to join the expedition, but
his health was so bad after his previous Arctic experiences
that he was not allowed to go.

The crew would number 25 men, and McClintock was
fortunate in securing the services of seventeen men with
Arctic experience, among them Lieutenant William R.
Hobson, who had served in the Arctic aboard the
Rattlesnake and *Plover* in 1853–54. Captain Allen Young,
a mercantile marine officer, came as the ship's master,
and donated £500 to the expedition's funds. McClintock's
younger brother – Dr Alfred Henry McClintock, a distinguished surgeon – recommended Dr David Walker for the

position of ship's surgeon. Carl Petersen, who had served with both Penny and Kane, would serve with McClintock as interpreter and dog-driver. Petersen perhaps voiced the opinion of all the crew when he said, 'McClintock I know – with him I will serve.' Petty Officer William Harvey joined the *Fox* as chief quartermaster. He had served aboard the *Resolute* in 1850–51, the *North Star* in 1852–53 and the *Phoenix* in 1854.

The early months of summer 1857 passed in a whirlwind of preparations. McClintock travelled to Aberdeen to view and re-register the *Fox*. In many ways, she was quite unsuitable for the planned expedition. Built by Messrs Hall and Company of Aberdeen for Sir Richard Sutton, the *Fox* had been on one cruise to the coast of Norway before being sold to Lady Franklin for £2,000. At 177 tons, she was tiny, and the men of Hall and Company now worked frantically to refit and strengthen her for Arctic service, attaching steel plates to her bows. The *Fox*, McClintock was assured, would be ready for sea by the end of May.

During the next few weeks, he shuttled between Aberdeen and London, taking occasional trips to the naval yards at Chatham and Deptford. The Admiralty – in a belated display of generosity – had agreed to supply both equipment and provisions for the expedition. McClintock was fortunate in that Captain Austin was in charge at Deptford, and he assisted McClintock with his preparations. All kinds of supplies were dispatched to Aberdeen – medicines, chronometers, navigational instruments, charts, Ordnance Board rifles, ammunition, Arctic clothing and rations, including more than 6,600 pounds of pemmican.

McClintock was obliged to undertake a round of visits and dinners, lobbying for support and funds from members of the Royal Geographical Society and the Royal Society. He made a speech at the Royal Geographical

Society annual dinner on 25 May, and later dined with the renowned African explorer, Dr David Livingstone. McClintock was elected as a member of the Victoria Yacht Club, the Cowes Royal Yacht Squadron and the Harwich Yacht Club, under whose flag the *Fox* would sail.

Worryingly, work on the *Fox* was taking longer than had been expected, prompting McClintock to return to Aberdeen in the hope of speeding up the work. Upon his return to London for the royal levee of 18 June 1857 he was presented to Queen Victoria by Lord Wrottesley, president of the Royal Society. Then it was back to Aberdeen, where Lady Franklin and her niece, Sophia Cracroft, arrived to observe final preparations. Lady Franklin had so far raised £10,412, and estimated that a further £7,000 would be required to cover future expenses. She signed a deed of indemnity, which freed McClintock from all liabilities and expenses, and also indicated a wish to sign ownership of the *Fox* over to him, an offer he declined. Furthermore, McClintock – in common with most of the officers – stated that he would forgo all pay for the duration of the expedition.

By this time, McClintock had finalised his plans for the expedition. He intended to search King William Island and the area between the mouths of the Coppermine River and the Great Fish River. He suggested to Lady Franklin that should the men of the Admiralty continue to grumble, she could point out that he intended to survey unknown coastline as well as investigating the possibility of achieving a Northwest Passage through Peel Sound.

After a final lunch aboard the *Fox*, Lady Franklin bade her farewells and was cheered ashore by the crew. McClintock put to sea, and by midnight on 1 July 1857 the *Fox* had passed Duncansby Head, bound for the Arctic.

CHAPTER THIRTEEN

Arctic Fox

Soon after departure the *Fox* ran aground off the Pentland Firth. It was an inauspicious beginning. McClintock sent a letter to Lady Franklin on 2 July 1857 giving some indication of the trouble. He wrote, 'Chief quartermaster was left behind, which is no loss I fancy.'[60]

McClintock took the *Fox* northwards, intending to put in to various ports on Greenland with a view to buying sledge-dogs, and to securing the services of dog-drivers and interpreters. During the course of the first days at sea he was imbued with a new sense of urgency. One of the crew, Michael Lewis, became seriously ill and was spitting blood. Dr Walker, the surgeon, informed McClintock that they must reach a port quickly so that Lewis could be returned for proper medical care. McClintock headed for southern Greenland, but found the seas off the coast choked with ice. Determined to push the tiny *Fox* through, he remained on deck for 60 hours straight, finally negotiating his way into Frederickshaab.

The journey had been a tense one, the little ship being rattled by the impact of large icebergs against her hull. Yet the emergency was not over. McClintock learned from Dr Rink, the Danish inspector at southern Greenland, that there were no ships leaving from Frederickshaab in the near future. This news prompted a rush to Godhavn to catch the schooner *Neptune*, which was about to sail for Copenhagen. On 31 July 1857 the *Fox* put into Godhavn (sometimes referred to as Lievely), where the ailing Lewis was transferred aboard *Neptune*, and where sledge-dogs were purchased.

The next call was to Disco Fjord, where the services of Anton Christian were secured; he would act as inter-preter, dog-driver and seal hunter. McClintock then had to negotiate the Waigat Sound, the narrow channel that separated Disco from Greenland. Here, he paused to take advantage of Rittenbenk Kolbrott, a seam of coal on the Disco side of the channel. The crew of the *Fox* dug out more than 7 tons of coal, and loaded it aboard ship – an extremely dangerous exercise, as large masses of ice disgorging into the Waigat could have severely damaged the *Fox*. But McClintock considered the coal to be crucial and the risk worthwhile. The *Fox* made final calls at the small coastal towns of Proven and Upernavik, from where the crew's last mail was dispatched and where McClintock also bought more sledge-dogs.

Heading out to sea he was now determined to take the *Fox* through the treacherous waters of Melville Bay. This was never an easy operation and the conditions in 1857 were the worst yet recorded. Whaling ships had turned back without even making the attempt, but McClintock could not afford to do so. Finding the ice densely packed, he soon realised that his tiny ship would not be able to force a way through. By the end of August he had pushed his way 110 miles across the bay. In another 60 miles or so he would reach the 'North Water'. He later wrote of being able to see only 'close heavy pack' to the west and, by the beginning of September, it had

The Fox beset in the ice of Baffin Bay, June 1858; photograph by Dr David Walker.

The Fox *beset in ice close to Greenland*
in the winter of 1857–58.

become obvious that the *Fox* would be beset in the pack
and would face an uncomfortable winter being carried
gradually southwards in the pack ice.

As before, McClintock endeavoured to keep his crew
distracted during winter. There were instructional classes
and festivities, and when weather and ice conditions
permitted, the men took exercise on the floes or practised
building ice huts. Yet there was no concealing the fact
that the *Fox* was nothing more than a minuscule collection of beams and spars adrift in a mass of Arctic ice.

During 250 days trapped in the ice, the *Fox* drifted
more than 1,190 miles down Baffin Bay and out into Davis
Strait. In late April 1858 the ship finally broke free from
the ice, but only after a terrifying ordeal. As she reached
the edge of the ice field, the swell of the sea became more
apparent. McClintock struggled to control the *Fox* as she
was tossed about in the waves. The sea was full of ice

hummocks and larger bergs, some over 70 feet high. For two days the tiny vessel was thrown about in a sea choked with these deadly bergs, an ordeal only brought to an end when the *Fox* broke free on 26 April – Easter Sunday.

The *Fox* had been caught in the ice for over eight months, but McClintock announced that they would immediately head north again to Greenland, and then make another attempt on Melville Bay. By 28 April he had brought the *Fox* to Holsteinsborg, from where he wrote a report for Lady Franklin in which he described their 242 days beset in the ice:

> During the autumn and up to the end of winter, when it became quite dark, nearly 60 seals were shot by the officers. Again on the return of light, about the end of January, seals were seen and latterly several of them were shot, in all 71, being sufficient to feed over 30 dogs over the winter and supply us with oil for the ship's use. Although bear or their tracks were seen in every month, only three were shot, one bear being hotly pursued by our dogs but he managed to wound four of them and make his escape. Very few fox tracks were seen and only one fox shot. On occasion a Dovekie in its winter plumage would reward the sportsman. In the month of May Narwhals were seen returning north.

He wrote of how the men practised building snow huts:

> At first a party of four men were fully occupied for four hours in hutting themselves. Latterly they could do so in half an hour.

McClintock concluded:

> Notwithstanding the total want of game and such objects of interest as the land alone can supply, and more than all the monotony of a winter under such depressing circumstances, the health of our small crew has been most excellent. I regret, however, that we have not been exempt from accidents; on the 2nd December, Robert Scott, leading stoker, fell down a hatchway, fracturing several ribs and receiving other internal injuries, which led to his death two days subsequently. How deeply impressive his funeral was on that wild December night, all who witnessed it will long remember. For their zealous good will and hearty devotion to the cause, I am indeed greatly indebted to every officer and man in the ship.[61]

When drawing up his plans for the expedition, McClintock had expressed his determination to avoid being beset in the ice. This delay was a serious blow to him and, from Holsteinsborg, he wrote another letter to Lady Franklin outlining his thoughts:

> The heading of this letter alone will explain to you that we did not reach Lancaster Sound last year, nor winter in a position to be useful, but this however is the worst that has befallen us . . . It is true that a year, an unfortunate year, has been lost, but it is a great consolation to know that we have more reason to hope for success now, in as much as we are very

early in the field and are ready to follow up
this advantage.[62]

By mid-May he was back at Godhavn, from where he
hired another Inuit dog-driver. On 26 May the *Fox* re-
entered the Waigat Sound, where more coal was dug out.
Upernivik was reached on 31 May. During this period
McClintock made contact with the crews of whalers off
Greenland in the hope of getting some useful information. He later wrote of how Captain Todd of the whaler
Lord Gambier told him of a rumour of a wreck in Pond's
Bay on the north of Baffin Island. The captains of the
whalers he encountered all proved to be incredibly generous, providing the *Fox* with fresh stores of beef, vegeta-
bles and coal, and always refusing payment of any kind.
Off Upernivik, British, Danish and American whalers were
encountered, and Captain Parker of the *Emma* donated
200 gallons of beer that he had brewed for them.

In a letter to Lady Franklin, McClintock wrote of the
reception his interpreter Carl Petersen received from the
Greenlanders:

> All Greenland is astonished at the wonderful
> voyages and unlooked for reappearance of Carl
> Petersen. They regard him as a sort of Flying
> Dutchman and listen with open mouths to his
> wonderful stories. There is but one opinion in
> Greenland and that is that he saved Kane's
> expedition. I like him very much.[63]

He concluded by remarking on the 'rumours from Pond's
Bay – very conflicting. I hope soon to get to the bottom
of them'.

By the start of June a new attempt was underway to

force the *Fox* through Melville Bay. Though weather conditions were much better this season, an anxious period was spent off Buchan Island when the *Fox* ran aground on a rock. Later in the day she drifted off with the rising tide. Once released from this dangerous situation, the *Fox* headed to Pond's Bay, where Inuit were interviewed about Franklin and his men. Nothing was known – a dreadful disappointment, especially as rumours from among the whalers had spoken of a wreck here. The Inuit had no knowledge of Franklin's ships or even those of Belcher's abandoned squadron. One old Inuit woman at Button Point did have memories of two wrecks that had been washed up around 25 miles away, though she estimated they had been discovered 30 years earlier. Nevertheless, McClintock made the journey to the Inuit settlement to examine the wood and metal fragments. Their apparent age satisfied him that the Inuit woman was correct in her opinion that these were earlier wrecks, and he supposed they may have been whalers.

McClintock spent the next week travelling by dog-sledge in order to talk with the Pond's Bay Inuit. He met with two local chiefs who amazed him by sketching accurate maps of the area. They also remembered wrecks and confirmed these had arrived on the coast over 30 years earlier. The Inuit stated that when they were still boys two ships had been beached to the south of Pond's Bay, about five days' journey by dog-sledge to the south of Button Point. They also remembered that a third wreck had washed up near Cape Bay, and they believed this to have been older still. None of these wrecks could have been the *Erebus* and *Terror*, and McClintock assumed they were the whalers that Parry had reported missing during his second expedition of 1819–20. Both Inuit chiefs had accurate memories of Parry's previous visit, and had even heard of Rae's expedition to Repulse Bay. Nevertheless, McClintock sadly concluded that 'The rumours of the Fish River Party from *Erebus* and *Terror* has not reached these people.'

Fox continued westwards, and the voyage was not without incident. At Navy Board Inlet, the depot was checked. Later, McClintock made a fascinating remark in a letter to Lady Franklin. He spoke of a rumour that an Inuit had found these stores and had eaten some of the food, only to be poisoned by it.[64] Could this support later claims that Franklin and his men had perished from consuming contaminated tinned food? Further incident occurred on 11 August 1858, just off Cape Riley, when a seaman named Hampton fell overboard. McClintock jumped into the icy porridge of the sea to rescue him.

On reaching Beechey Island, a marble memorial tablet was erected. Dedicated to Franklin, Crozier and the officers and men of *Terror* and *Erebus*, it had been commissioned by Lady Franklin and taken as far as Godhavn in 1855, from where McClintock had carried it to Beechey Island. A short service was conducted – a poignant moment since, by this time, it was known that Franklin and his men were dead. While Lady Franklin and others occasionally voiced the hope that perhaps some had survived and were living with the Inuit, in their hearts they knew this was unlikely. The erection of the memorial tablet obliged McClintock to face an unpalatable truth – the best he could hope for was to recover the bodies of Franklin and his men.

On 16 August – the ship's stores having been replenished from the large depot on Beechey Island – the *Fox* sailed for the depot at Cape Hotham. McClintock examined this in the vain hope that it had been reached by Franklin's men, and that they had taken supplies and left a message. Finding the depot to be intact, he took the *Fox* down Peel Sound, the channel disregarded by several search expeditions as they had found it choked with ice. After taking the *Fox* some 25 miles into the channel, the way was blocked by thick pack ice. McClintock retraced his route and headed southwards through Prince Regent Inlet, and made it halfway through Bellot Strait before being blocked by the ice. He decided to wait here in the hope that the weather conditions would improve and allow the *Fox* to pass through the channel.

For over a month he remained in this spot, making repeated attempts to force his way through Bellot Strait. On 15 September a way was forced through, and McClintock took the *Fox* further south before being stopped again off a small island, near Cape Bird. He dubbed it Pemmican Rock, and established a large depot there.

Finding the way blocked by closely packed ice, McClintock inched the *Fox* onwards until 27 September, when he lodged her in a small harbour on the west coast of Boothia, later named Port Kennedy. As new ice began to form around the vessel, he realised this was where they would be spending the winter of 1858–59 – a disappointment, as he had hoped to bring the *Fox* even further south to ensure shorter journeys for his sledge parties in the spring of 1859.

As winter passed, McClintock made plans for the following year's searches. He and his men would explore the west coast of Boothia, King William Island and as far as the mouth of Back's Great Fish River.

Back in 1854 Rae and King of the Hudson's Bay Company had gathered the first information concerning the fate of Franklin. Now, four years on, McClintock's sledge parties were about to unearth the first, and only, documentary account left by Franklin's men.

CHAPTER FOURTEEN

Beset in the Arctic

McClintock planned to undertake extensive searches in 1859. Accordingly, prior to the onset of winter 1858 he undertook preliminary reconnaissance and lay in depots. With twelve men and 22 dogs at his disposal, he sent out sledge parties to carry out this initial work and to make contact with the local Inuit population.

The men laboured to establish a series of depots on Arcedeckne Island, from where Hobson took supplies to be used for the establishment of depots further to the west. During the months of February and March 1859 Allen Young made a series of journeys carrying supplies for a depot on the north shore of Prince of Wales Island. In mid-March he went to Fury Beach to obtain a supply of sugar from the stores left there in 1824. Taking two dog-sledges and assisted only by an Inuit and a sailor, he covered the 400-mile round trip in record time, and brought 8 hundredweight of sugar back to the *Fox*.

McClintock next decided to carry out an extended reconnaissance in the direction of the magnetic North Pole. He left the *Fox* on 17 February with a dog-team, travelling with one sailor and the interpreter, Carl Petersen. His ultimate aim was to make contact with the local Inuit to learn if they had information regarding Franklin and his men. The journey was extremely tough, not least because they had left their tent behind so as to travel light. Instead of a tent, McClintock planned to build a snow hut every night, as he had seen the Inuit do. Unused to such activity, it took an exhausting two hours each night to complete the task.

By 1 March they had reached the magnetic North Pole, where they met four Inuit returning from a seal hunt. Next day around 40 Inuit men, women and children came from their village to meet McClintock's party. Nearly all the Inuit carried some relic of the *Erebus* and *Terror*, and several told how two ships had been beset in ice out at sea. McClintock traded with them for several relics before retracing his steps to the *Fox*.

In the course of a 26-day journey, his party had travelled over 360 miles, surveying the last unknown coast of North America, and making crucial discoveries about Franklin and the fabled Northwest Passage. McClintock had discovered that the only Northwest Passage that could be navigated by ships lay to the east side of King William Island. While McClure had completed a Northwest Passage and Franklin's ships had been beset in one, McClintock had found a navigable, open-water passage.

On his return to the *Fox*, he was faced with a new problem. Mr Brand, the second engineer, was seized by a sudden apoplectic fit and died. The first engineer, Scott, had died the previous winter and McClintock now had no one properly qualified to run the ship's steam engine. He put this problem to the back of his mind with a view to tackling it when the time came to leave Port Kennedy.

During the rest of March 1859 McClintock and his officers made their final plans for that year's sledging expeditions. Depots had been laid down in the directions

they intended to travel. Having made contact with the
Inuit and taking into account the relics he had bought,
McClintock knew they were searching in the right area.
In addition to searching for evidence of the Franklin expedition, he also intended to complete a survey of the Parry
Islands. Three sledges, each with a five-man team – led
by Hobson, Young and himself – were to be assisted by
auxiliary sledges pulled by dog-teams. Hobson was to
search the north coast of King William Island before crossing to Gateshead Island and Victoria Island. Young was
to complete a survey of the southern coast of Prince of
Wales Island before searching the area from Four Rivers
Bay to Bellot Strait. McClintock intended to travel southwards to Montreal Island in the mouth of Back's Great
Fish River, an area where Rae reported that the Inuit had
found the bodies of some of Franklin's men. McClintock
then intended to return via King William Island. He
suspected that the most important evidence regarding
the fate of Franklin would be found here, and his plans
allowed for searches by both himself and Hobson. The
routes of these searches would also allow them to
complete the survey of the Parry Islands.

On 2 April 1859 the three teams set out. McClintock
was accompanied by Petersen, Alexander Thompson and
two other sailors, named Carey and Hampton. Thompson had previously served aboard *Resolute* during the
Belcher expedition and had accompanied McClintock
during his 1854 dog-sledge journey. Lieutenant Hobson
and his team travelled with McClintock as far as Cape
Victoria. Here, they parted, Hobson crossing over to Cape
Felix on King William Island.

Hobson was to have a short but very fruitful journey.
He reached Cape Felix on 2 May, where he found a large
cairn of stones. Disappointingly, a search of the cairn

Commencement of McClintock's exploring parties,
2 April 1859.

produced nothing but a blank piece of paper. Scattered
around the cairn, however, was ample evidence that
Franklin's men had passed this way: the remains of a
campsite and, scattered among the abandoned tents,
clothes, tools and utensils. Soon afterwards, Hobson and
his men found another cairn, but on examination found
it contained nothing. On the morning of 6 May yet
another cairn was found, but this held only a broken pick-
axe and an empty document canister. Around 4 miles
further south, Hobson came across the remains of another
campsite. A large quantity of equipment was lying alongside a cairn of stones, and among the loose stones of the
cairn, Hobson found, inside a tin container, a document
– a standard printed form supplied to discovery ships.
Written in the margins, however, was a handwritten
message:

28 of May 1847
H.M.S.hips *Erebus* and *Terror* Wintered in the
Ice in Lat. 70° 5' N Long. 98° 23' W
Having wintered in 1846–7 at Beechey Island
in Lat. 74° 43' 28" N. Long. 91° 39' 15" W. after
having ascended Wellington Channel to Lat
77° and returned by the West side of Corn-
wallis Island.
Sir John Franklin commanding the expedition.
All well.
Party consisting of 2 officers and 6 men left
the ships on Monday 24th. May 1847
Gm. Gore, Lieut.
Chas. F. Des Vœux, Mate[65]

Hobson immediately noted an error: the *Erebus* and
Terror had wintered at Beechey Island in 1845–46, not
1846–47 as stated on the note. Otherwise, this message
was positive in that all were well in May 1847. In the hope
of finding further information, Hobson and his men
continued southwards but, as the weather worsened, all
the members of the team began to fall ill. By 22 May they
had reached their furthest-south. Leaving a cairn and a
record for McClintock, Hobson turned his men northwards, heading back to the *Fox*. En route they found a
large boat on the beach, and on 28 May a small cairn was
found at Back's Bay containing a second document –
again, the standard printed form. The handwritten
message from Gore and Des Vœux was repeated on this
form, together with a later, and frightening, addition
by Captain James Fitzjames. This second message read:

25th April 1848 H.M.Ships *Terror* and *Erebus*
were deserted on the 22nd April. 5 leagues

NNW of this having been beset since 12th Septr 1846. The officers and crews consisting of 105 souls – under the command of Captain F.R.M. Crozier landed here – in Lat 69° 37' 42" Long 98° 41'.

This paper was found by Lt. Irving under the cairn supposed to have been built by Sir James Ross in 1831, 4 miles to the Northward – where it had been deposited by the late Commander Gore in June 1847. Sir James Ross' pillar has not however been found, and the paper has been transferred to this position which is that in which Sir J. Ross' pillar was erected

Sir John Franklin died on the 11th June 1847 and the total loss by deaths in the Expedition has been to this date 9 officers and 15 men.
James Fitzjames, Captain HMS *Erebus*
FRM Crozier Captain and Senior offr.
and start on tomorrow 26th for Backs Fish River[66]

Finally, after eleven years and dozens of search expeditions, here was a record of what had become of Franklin and his men.

Hobson now returned to the cairn where the first message had been found to carry out another, fruitless, search. Turning for home, Hobson's team reached the *Fox* on 14 June, having been absent for 74 days. In essence, the Franklin mystery was now solved. The messages found by Hobson told in basic form the sad history of the expedition. These two documents remain the only written records ever found from the expedition.

H.M.S.*hips* Erebus *and* Terro
{ *Wintered in the Ice in*

28 of May 1847 { Lat. 70°5' N. Long. 98°23' W

Having wintered in 1846—7 at Beechey Island

in Lat 74° 43. 28" N. Long 91°39. 15" W After having

ascended Wellington Channel to Lat 77° and returned
by the West side of Cornwallis Island.

Commander.

Sir John Franklin commanding the Expedition
all well

WHOEVER finds this paper is requested to forward it to the Secretary of the Admiralty, London, *with a note of the time and place at which it was found:* or, if more convenient, to deliver it for that purpose to the British Consul at the nearest Port.

QUINCONQUE trouvera ce papier est prié d'y marquer le tems et lieu où il l'aura trouvé, et de le faire parvenir au plutot au Secrétaire de l'Amirauté Britannique à Londres.

CUALQUIERA que hallare este Papel, se le súplica de enviarlo al Secretario del Almirantazgo, en Londrés, con una nota del tiempo y del lugar en donde so halló.

EEN ieder die dit Papier mogt vinden, wordt hiermede versogt, om het zelve, ten spoedigste, te willen zenden aan den Heer Minister van de Marine der Nederlanden in 's Gravenhage, of wel aan den Secretaris den Britsche Admiraliteit, te London, en daar by te voegen eene Nota, inhoudende de tyd en de plaats alwaar dit Papier is gevonden geworden.

FINDEREN af dette Papiir ombedes, naar Leilighed gives, at sende samme til Admiralitets-Secretairen i London, eller nærmeste Embedsmand i Danmark, Norge, eller Sverrig. Tiden og Stedet hvor dette er fundet önskes venskabeligt paategnet.

WER diesen Zettel findet, wird hierdurch ersucht denselben an den Secretair des Admiralitets in London einzusenden, mit gefälliger Angabe an welchen Ort und zu welcher Zeit er gefunden worden ist.

Party consisting of 2 Officers and 6 Men
left the Ships on Sunday 24th May 1847

Gm Gore Lieut
Chas F Des Vœux Mate

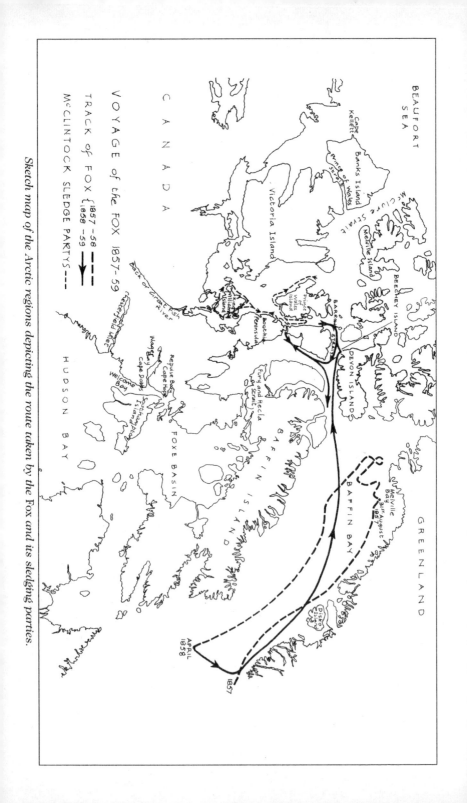

Sketch map of the Arctic regions depicting the route taken by the Fox and its sledging parties.

CHAPTER FIFTEEN

A Melancholy Tragedy

While Hobson was making his historic discovery, McClintock was driving southwards, reaching Matty Island on 4 May, only to find a deserted village. Wishing to communicate with the local Inuit, he returned to the coast of King William Island, where he came across an inhabited snow-hut village. The Inuit here were in possession of silver plate which had belonged to Franklin, Crozier and other officers of the missing expedition. McClintock purchased the items from the Inuit, who told him that the wreck of a ship lay about four days' march away. They also told him how, many years before, a large party of white men had left the ship and headed southwards, and how 'they fell down and died as they walked along'.[67]

Having decided to head for the mouth of the Great Fish River, McClintock reached Point Ogle on 12 May. In the face of an Arctic gale, Montreal Island was reached on 15 May, where a search was undertaken in the hope of finding a cairn with a record encased within it. Sadly, only debris was found – perhaps the remains of one of the ship's boats that had been dismantled by the Inuit for its metal and wood. McClintock also noted the almost total absence of game – significant in that he was travelling over the same ground that Franklin's men had covered and at the same time of year. Later in the summer the deer migration would begin and there would be ample opportunities to get fresh meat. But the unfortunate crews of *Erebus* and *Terror* had been forced to travel in this barren landscape at the worst time of year for hunting game.

On 24 May McClintock once again led his party across the sea to King William Island. His goal now was to return to the *Fox* by way of the western coast of the island, traversing the same shore Franklin's men had walked in their trek southwards. His men explored the coastline with keen attention, and kept a watch out to sea in the hope of sighting the ship that the Inuit had spoken of. On 25 May a skeleton – held together with fragments of clothing – was found on top of a gravel ridge. Judging by the clothes, McClintock deduced the man had been an officer's steward. Though later there was some confusion concerning the identity of this body, McClintock identified these remains as those of Harry Peglar, captain of the foretop in the *Terror*.

McClintock and his men reached Cape Herschel – discovered by Simpson in 1839 – and searched the large cairn of stones placed there by Simpson. McClintock was sure that Franklin's men would have found this large and imposing cairn, and placed some sort of record within it. The cairn was carefully examined and the surrounding soil excavated, but nothing was found. Noting some damage to the cairn, McClintock reckoned it had been examined by Inuit who may have found a record and, deeming it worthless, thrown it away. This might also explain why all but one of the cairns examined by Hobson had been empty.

About 12 miles from Cape Herschel, McClintock came upon the cairn and record that Hobson had left for him.

This new intelligence dovetailed with the information the Inuit had given him, leading McClintock to conclude that the coast he was now exploring was the correct one; the discovery by Hobson of one of Franklin's boats on the shoreline confirmed it.

McClintock was now keen to examine this boat. On reaching the western extreme of King William Island on 29 May, he christened it Cape Crozier, in honour of his fellow countryman. On 30 May McClintock stood alongside the boat Hobson had discovered. His description of the site is typically detailed:

> A vast quantity of tattered clothing was lying in her, and this we first examined. Not a single article bore the name of its former owner. The boat was cleared out and carefully swept that nothing might escape us. The snow was then removed from about her but nothing whatever was found. This boat measured 28 feet long and 7 feet 3 inches wide; she was built with a view to lightness and light draught of water, and evidently equipped with the utmost care for the ascent of the Great Fish River.[68]

He noted that the weight of the boat was around 7–800 pounds, and that it had been placed on a sledge weighing around 650 pounds. Laden with provisions, the crews of *Erebus* and *Terror* had toiled to drag this incredible weight to the south, all the time ailing due to a lack of food. He continued:

> But all these were after observations; there was in the boat that which transfixed us with awe, viz., portions of two human skeletons!

One was that of a slight young person; the other of a large, strongly made, middle-aged man. The former was found in the bow of the boat, but in too much of a disturbed state to enable Hobson to judge whether the sufferer had died there; large and powerful animals, probably wolves, had destroyed much of this skeleton, which may have been that of an officer.[69]

He described the second body:

The other skeleton was in a somewhat more perfect state; it lay across the boat, under the after-thwart and was enveloped in cloths and furs. This would seem to have been the survivor of the two men whose remains were lying in the boat. Close beside it were two double-barrelled guns – one barrel in each loaded and cocked – standing muzzle upwards against the boat's side. It may be imagined with what deep interest these sad relics were scrutinised and how anxiously every fragment of clothing was turned over in search of pockets and pocket-books, or even names.[70]

Indeed, the area around this boat was strewn with all kinds of equipment. Hobson reckoned that the men pulling this boat had realised they were fighting for their lives, and had abandoned all superfluous equipment. McClintock catalogued the findings: boots and clothes, ammunition, toiletries, watches and a quantity of silver inscribed with the initials or family crests of Franklin's officers. A poignant collection of reading material included Oliver Goldsmith's *The Vicar of Wakefield*, and a much used and annotated Bible. Also found were jackets of a New Testament and a *Book of Common Prayer*. Had the pages been torn out and used to light fires, he wondered. A small quantity of tea and around 40 pounds of chocolate were the only items of food in the vicinity. The only evidence of food having been consumed was a single discarded pemmican tin.

These discoveries puzzled McClintock, and posed as many questions as they answered. Though he reckoned that a party of twenty or 30 men had been attached to the boat, he found only the remains of two, and there was no evidence of any graves in the vicinity. Equally baffling was the position of the sledge and boat. On this, McClintock later wrote:

> I was astonished to find that the sledge was directed to the N.E., exactly for the next point of land for which we ourselves were travelling! The position of the abandoned boat is about 50 miles – as a sledge would travel – from Point Victory, and therefore 65 miles from the position of the ships; also it is 70 miles from the skeleton of the steward, and 150 miles from Montreal Island; it is moreover in the depth of a wide bay, where by crossing over 10 or 12 miles of very low land, a great saving of distance would be effected, the route by the coastline being 40 miles. A little reflection led me to satisfy my own mind at least that this boat was *returning to the ships*. In no other way can I account for two men having been left in her, than by supposing the party were unable to drag the boat further, and that these

RELICS OF THE FRANKLIN EXPEDITION.

Snelling.   Common Clay Pipe.   Seal.   Star of Harland's Stoker.   Mittee.   Tin Can.   Snow-Goggles.

LIEUT. HOBSON, R.N.

LIEUTENANT WILLIAM ROBERT HOBSON, R.N., is the only son of the late Captain William Robert Hobson, R.N., distinguished alike as a naval officer and as the first Governor of New Zealand and the founder of its capital, Auckland. Lieutenant Hobson entered the service in the year 1845. He was mate of the *Rattlesnake* in her expedition to Behring's Straits as relieving-ship to the *Enterprise* and *Investigator*, and gained his first experience of Arctic travelling whilst serving in her. He was made Lieutenant early in 1855, and served on board the *Majestic* during the Baltic campaign of that year. In 1857 he volunteered to accompany Captain M'Clintock in the *Fox*. How well he performed the duties he undertook is already known to the public.

THE YACHT "FOX" ENTERING LIEVELY HARBOUR, DISCO, GREENLAND.

Few spots within the arctic zone are invested with deeper interest than the Danish settlement of Lievely, on the island of Disco, situated on the west coast of Greenland, at the northern extreme of Davis's Straits. The settlement consists of a few wooden houses and numerous Esquimaux huts, built on a low projecting tongue of land which incloses the long fiord of Gothaven. From this outpost of

civilisation have sailed in modern days all our numerous arctic expeditions of discovery as well as search. Sir John Ross, Parry, Franklin, Austen, Penny, Belcher, and, lastly, M'Clintock, have all been there; have all acknowledged the kindness and hospitality of the worthy Danes therein located; and most of them, on their return from their adventurous voyages within the ice-girt regions north of Disco, have visited it for the purpose of refitting before pushing homeward across the Atlantic. Disco was well known to the hardy navigators of Great Elizabeth's day—Davis, Baffin, and Frobisher; and, from the existence of Scandinavian relics in its neighbourhood, there can be no doubt that it was by way of this part of Greenland that the Norsemen of olden time were led on to the discovery of America, as Icelandic records relate, centuries before it was reached by Christopher Columbus. Iceland, from Norway, we have in the Shetlands, Iceland, and Greenland, a series of stepping-stones which naturally led those bold seamen to the great continent of the western hemisphere.

THE "FOX" WINTERING IN THE PACK.

SAILING from Lievely, in 1858, the gallant little *Fox* reached the mobile ice in Melville Bay too late to force her way through it into the open water, which generally exists at the entrance of Lancaster Sound. After a fruitless battle with insurmountable obstacles, the *Fox* was suddenly caught in the winter-grip of the packed ice, a fearfully dangerous position, which all navigators in those icy seas strain every nerve to avoid, and, fast in its icy embrace, the hundreds of gallant men under Captain M'Clintock could only resign themselves to their fate, and trust in an Overruling Providence for safety.

The winter pack-ice of Lancaster Sound and Baffin's Bay rolls steadily towards the Atlantic throughout the darkness and cold of an arctic winter. No water is seen, but the action of a polar current flowing south sweeps the millions and millions of tons of ice which incumber its surface in one resistless stream into the frozen bosom of the Atlantic, there to be broken up, thawed, and dispersed along the shores of North America as far down as the Bermudas. Of course, as this vast stream of packed ice passes down Baffin's Bay it meets all descriptions of impediments. Sometimes long chains or reefs of grounded icebergs lie athwart the stream; it matters not, the pack is merely shivered into fragments and passed through the interstices, or the icebergs, large as they are, are rolled or moved along in the embrace of the resistless packed ice. Sometimes the channel contracts, as in Davis's Straits, fearful pressure takes place, the pack breaks up and cracks in all directions, and mass mounts on top of mass until the ice can find a vent. The reader can therefore

RELICS OF THE FRANKLIN EXPEDITION.—SEE SUPPLEMENT, PAGE 381.

1. Pen-jib.   b. Boat-hook to find in boat.   e. Blade of paddle.   4. Case, in which the M.S. was found.   5. Copy of the "View of Wakefield."   6. Snuff found under neck of skeleton.   7. Gun, one barrel loaded.
8. Chronometer found in boat, belonging to Sir J. Franklin.   9. Piece of rope.   10. Implement obtained from the Esquimaux.   11. Sextant.   12. Top of gun-case.   13. Knives found in boat.   14. Knocked plate of tryfu.
15. Pair of spectacles.   16. Powder-flask.   17. Implement obtained from the Esquimaux.   18. Clothes-brush.   19. Pair of Goggles.   20. Arrows.   21. Snuff-box.

two men, not being able to keep pace with their shipmates, were therefore left by them supplied with such provisions as could be spared, to last them until the return of the others from the ship with a fresh stock. Whether it was the intention of this boat party to await the result of another season in the ships, or to follow the track of the main body to the Great Fish River, is now a matter of conjecture. It seems more probable that they fully intended to revisit the boat, not only on account of the two men left in charge of it but also to obtain the chocolate, the five watches, and many other small articles which would otherwise scarcely have been left in her.[71]

He concluded that this party had 'overrated its strength', and that the men were forced to return for more food, perhaps perishing en route to the ships or on their return to the boat. It was a depressing insight into how Franklin's expedition had disintegrated into smaller groups, and how these had in turn disappeared as the men died one by one from hunger.

Leaving his grim discoveries behind him, McClintock turned his team towards the *Fox*. On 2 June they reached Point Victory, where an inlet was named after Captain Collinson and a bay after Captain Washington, hydrographer to the navy. McClintock later stated that 'all the intermediate coastline, along which the retreating crews performed their fearful death march, is sacred to their names alone'.

Around the cairn at Point Victory, more abandoned equipment was found – clothes, shovels, cooking stoves and a medicine chest, among a scatter of other debris.

They continued northwards and, in rapidly deteriorating weather, reached the *Fox* on 19 June. McClintock's team had been absent from the ship for 78 days and had travelled over 920 miles, surveying around 800 miles of new coastline.

McClintock's next pressing concern was to locate the sledge party of Captain Allen Young. Young had left the *Fox* on 7 April and had not yet returned. While McClintock was heading to Montreal Island, Young had sledged to Prince of Wales Island, and had attempted to reach Victoria Island. He had returned to Pemmican Rock to replenish his stores from the depot there, before travelling along the east coast of Prince of Wales Island and crossing to North Somerset, completing the survey of its west coast as far as Cape Bird. Young's party returned to Pemmican Rock on 27 June, where they met McClintock, who had sledged out in search of them. They had been absent for 82 days.

The exhausted sledge party, accompanied by McClintock, returned to the *Fox*. All that remained was for McClintock to extricate his ship and head for home, bearing the sad news of the fate of Franklin and his men.

CHAPTER SIXTEEN

A Bearer of Sad Tidings

As the last of Hobson's men rejoined the ship, McClintock knew he had to get the *Fox* and its crew out of the Arctic as soon as possible. They had found the evidence they had been searching for and there was no point in further delay. To add urgency to the situation, Dr Walker expressed serious doubts about the health of the men. One of the crew, Thomas Blackwell, had died of scurvy in early June, while Hobson and several others were also suffering from its ill effects.

During the remainder of July McClintock made preparations to leave. Several hunting trips were made, during which he employed the stalking techniques he had learned from the Inuit. He shot hares and wildfowl, and this diet of fresh meat improved the men's health to some degree. There was also the problem of the *Fox*'s engines. The engines had been dismantled when the *Fox* was secured in its winter harbour, but both of the ship's engineers were now dead. The first-class certificate in steam machinery McClintock had been awarded when still a young officer now proved a lifesaver. He spent several days reassembling the engines and eventually got them back in working order.

In early August 1859 a strengthening south-west wind began to move the ice offshore. On 10 August the *Fox* broke free from the ice, leaving Port Kennedy behind her forever. When the wind died down, McClintock had to make use of the engines, which initially caused some trouble. He later wrote:

> The wind now failed us and I experienced some little difficulty in the management of the engines and boiler; the latter primed so violently as to send hot water and steam over the top-gallant yard, to the dismay of Young, who was up there piloting the ship through the ice and who was, of course, very speedily compelled to descend from his eyrie: and the tail valve of the condenser by some means had got out of its seat, and admitted air to the condenser; but eventually we got the engines to work well, and steamed across Cresswell Bay during the night.[72]

Homeward bound, the *Fox* put in at Godhavn for mail before making for the English Channel, which McClintock reached on 20 September 1859. Having come ashore at Portsmouth, he hastened to London where he informed Admiralty officials of the outcome of what he termed the 'final searching expedition': 'Their Lordships will rejoice to hear that our endeavours to ascertain the fate of the Franklin Expedition have met with complete success.'[73] In a letter written to Lady Franklin from the United Service Club in London on 21 September 1859 he allowed himself to elaborate:

> I am sure that you entertained no high hopes

of survivors being found and this understood you will, I think, receive our news as good news. Brief records have been found but they tell us that the expedition wintered at Beechey Island after ascending Wellington Channel to Latitude 77° N. That they were beset in September 1846 off the west coast of King William's Land. Sir John Franklin died on 11 June 1847. The ships were abandoned nearly in the same place on 22 April 1848. The survivors under Crozier and Fitzjames numbered in all 105. They proceeded with boats on sledges to the Great Fish River.[74]

On the documents he had found, he commented:

I cannot help remarking to you, what instantly occurred to me on reading the records. That Sir John Franklin was not harassed by either want of success or forbodings of evil. It was the summer of 1847 which proved fatal to the crews of the expedition.[75]

In a letter to the Admiralty, McClintock told of the discovery of the written record and added:

Many deeply interesting relics of our lost countrymen have been picked up on the western shore of King William's Island and others obtained from the Esquimaux.[76]

Regarding the Inuit account of the fate of the ships, he forwarded their report of one ship being sunk while the other was forced onshore. McClintock added that the wreck had provided the Inuit with 'an almost inexhaustible mine of wealth'.

Despite his grim tidings, McClintock had returned to London to be treated as a hero. The *Fox* docked at Blackwell on 23 September, and a few days later the crew was paraded and McClintock awarded his men the Arctic Medal. He received the Freedom of the City of London and was entertained at a number of official dinners. Shortly after his return, he published his account of the expedition: *The Voyage of the* Fox *in the Arctic Seas in Search of Franklin and His Companions* (London, 1859). The book – dedicated to Lady Franklin – was an immediate success and quickly ran to several editions. It remains one of the most gripping and readable accounts of the Arctic expeditions of the period.

In October 1859, in an unexpected act of generosity, the Admiralty announced that the period McClintock had spent in command of the *Fox* would thereafter be counted as service aboard one of Her Majesty's ships. He would not, however, be awarded full pay. Parliament later granted an award of £5,000 to the officers and men of the *Fox*, of which McClintock's share was £1,500.

In October 1859 he organised a display of the Franklin relics in the United Service Club in London, and in a letter to the Admiralty, wrote of his hope that a 'national repository' would be opened to hold these relics, which were now 'preserved and opened for public inspection'. He also wrote to the families of several of Franklin's officers and men, informing them that he had found items belonging to their missing family members. The items were made available to families that wished to reclaim them.

Alongside these sad duties, McClintock found himself the focus of public attention and praise. He was awarded honorary degrees from the universities of Cambridge,

Lieutenant William R. Hobson and Leopold McClintock
on their return from the Fox expedition in 1859.

Oxford and Trinity College, Dublin.[77] This was somewhat ironic when one considers the poor education he had received as a youngster. On 31 October 1859 he was honoured with a formal dinner in his native Dundalk, and was presented with an illuminated address and a piece of silver. In his speech of thanks, he said he promised to

> Cherish it always, more than any other honour,
> as it comes from the town where I spent my
> youth, from the friends of my boyhood days,
> from my home.[78]

On 14 November 1859 he gave a lecture on the *Fox* voyage to the Royal Geographical Society. He was elected a Fellow of the Royal Geographical Society and awarded the society's Gold Medal. Yet it was typical of the man to later state that his proudest moment was when the crew of the *Fox* presented him with a gold chronometer:

> As long as I live it will remind me of that
> perfect harmony, that mutual esteem and
> goodwill, which made our ship's company a
> happy little community, and contributed
> materially to the success of the expedition.[79]

He was listed in the New Year's Honours of 1860,
Queen Victoria later carrying out the knighting cere-
mony with Lord Gough's sword; Gough was another
Victorian icon with Irish connections.

McClintock was fêted in Dublin and was the guest
of honour at a Dublin Castle dinner in January 1860. In
a letter of 22 January 1860 he wrote from 48 Hardwicke
Street in Dublin to Lady Franklin:

> The good people here are trying to make me
> believe that I am not the same individual that
> I was before I sailed in the *Fox*. I dined at the
> Lord Lieutenant's banquet yesterday: 102
> persons sat down together in St Patrick's Hall;
> it was really a splendid sight. The Lord Lieu-
> tenant introduced me to some of the Grandees
> and said 'we are quite proud of him'. He has
> wonderful tact in 'gammoning' us over here.[80]

CHAPTER SEVENTEEN

The Fate of Franklin

The months following his return in the *Fox* were ones of hectic activity, as McClintock found himself lauded in the press and treated by the public as a veritable hero. Why was he the focus of such attention? It could be argued that John Rae of the Hudson's Bay Company had preceded him with news of the fate of Franklin and his men. Yet Rae had become an unpopular bearer of bad tidings. The reports he had recorded from the Inuit suggested that the remnants of the Franklin expedition had indeed ended up near the mouth of the Great Fish River. He also brought less palatable news, repeating and publishing the Inuit stories of mutilated bodies and cannibalism. This story did not fit into the tapestry of myth that was already being woven around the facts to create the Franklin legend. The public could accept the story of the tragedy as it unfolded – provided it was a noble and heroic one.

The news McClintock brought back fitted nicely into this script and, indeed, he answered many of the public's questions about the affair. The document that Hobson had found on King William Island allowed him to illustrate the route and initial progress of the expedition.

Having passed their first winter at Beechey Island, *Erebus* and *Terror* had proceeded through Peel Sound before becoming beset to the northwest of King William Island. There the ships would remain. They were within 90 miles of known sea off the coast of Canada and from completing a Northwest Passage. Having already covered some 500 miles of previously unexplored waters, they must have been confident of proceeding during the next navigable season. As late as May 1847 the report stated that the crew were 'All well', and also noted that a sledge party had left the ship, commanded by Lieutenant Gore and Mate Des Vœux. McClintock assumed this party had explored the coasts of King William Island. The additions made to the document on 25 April 1848 by Crozier and Fitzjames told of the expedition's rapidly deteriorating situation. The ships were still beset, Sir John Franklin had died on 11 June 1847, and the expedition had so far lost nine officers and fifteen men. Commander Gore, who had written the 'All well' message just over a year before, was now described as the 'late Commander Gore'. Given their dire position, Crozier and Fitzjames were forced to take the surviving crew ashore and head south for the Great Fish River.

In the years that followed McClintock's discoveries, other explorers found new evidence and put more flesh on the bare bones of his story. A trail of graves, skeletons and debris from the expedition meanders down the coast from Point Victory on King William Island as far as the estuary of the Great Fish River. It has been surmised that around a third of those crews were unable to proceed beyond Terror Bay, where they were installed in an ad hoc tent hospital. At this point, Crozier split his party into two groups – one consisting of the sick and those who would care for them, the other comprised of those still

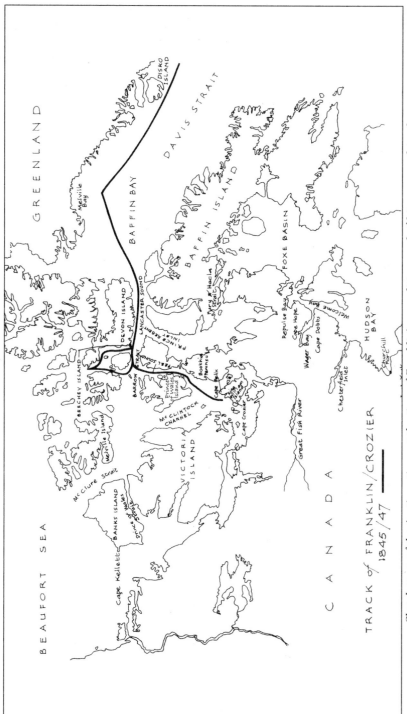

Sketch map of the Arctic regions at the time of Franklin's expedition, and of his supposed track.

able to march. Some of those left with the sick appear to have headed back to the ship for more supplies, and it is likely that the boat with the two skeletons found by Hobson and later examined by McClintock represented some of this party. Local Inuit later told of finding around 30 bodies at Terror Bay.

The second party of fitter men followed Crozier southwards, and many fell during the march, including Harry Peglar, whose body was found by McClintock near Cape Herschel. Several bodies were later found at Douglas Bay, while the remains of a campsite was discovered on the Piffer River, close to where a skeleton of an officer was found. In 1950 more skeletal remains were found on Todd Island, suggesting that some of the survivors were heading for the Adelaide Peninsula. Most of the remainder of Crozier's command are thought to have died at the aptly named Starvation Cove, while other members of the expedition reached Montreal Island before dying.

The Inuit told subsequent searchers of their interactions with the ill-fated expedition, and of how they traded seal meat with a party of around 40 starving men – the white men were living on any birds they could shoot. The Inuit told of finding the body of a large man on King William Island – he had a telescope and was perhaps an officer. They told of how one of the ships beset off Cape Crozier was crushed by the ice and sank. The other broke free and drifted southwards, and the Inuit boarded it as it drew close to the coast. On board, they found the decomposing body of a man – confirmation that some of the expedition crew had returned to the ship. It is now believed that this ship was later wrecked on the coast of O'Reilly Island, off the Adelaide Peninsula. The Inuit also reported hearing the gunshots of hunting parties in May 1850 – an indication of how long the last men had survived.

Yet the information gathered by Rae, McClintock and later explorers has only served to fuel the debate on the Franklin expedition, and there has been a consistent argument that something disastrous must have occurred to account for the loss of two ships and 129 officers and men. Before long, the canned rations were pinpointed as a possible source of the problem, some suggesting that the lead solder on the cans had poisoned the crew – leading to reduced mental powers and eventual death. This theory seemed to be backed up by twentieth-century investigations, when high levels of lead were found in some of the corpses. In the 1980s the corpses on Beechey Island were disinterred by an American expedition and subjected to post-mortems. Analysis of the bodies provided evidence of a high lead content. The theory falls apart, however, when one considers that only eleven per cent of the expedition's rations were tinned. Those taking issue with the lead-poison theory also point out that environmental factors in Industrial Revolution Britain would account for the high lead levels in the bodies. An outbreak of botulism has also been suggested, with the tinned rations again identified as the source, but there is no evidence whatsoever to support this theory.

The real reasons for the demise of Franklin and his men were probably much more straightforward and less fascinating. The expedition had been hastily organised as Sir John Barrow was keen to see the discovery of a Northwest Passage before he retired as second secretary of the Admiralty. Not enough attention had been given to the provisions and equipment for the expedition – there was simply not enough food and the clothing proved to be totally inadequate. The *Erebus* and *Terror* had steam engines fitted, and this reduced the space available to store provisions, a fact that had led to the misgivings of

Crozier. The addition of steam engines also deepened the draught of the ships, and this would have made it more difficult for them to negotiate shallow channels.

There was also the question of the man chosen to lead the expedition. Franklin had made his reputation as an overland explorer, and even then his first expedition had ended in near disaster. He had been dismissed as governor of Tasmania, and had ceaselessly lobbied the Admiralty in the belief that this command would rescue his tattered reputation. He had no experience of commanding a sea expedition, he was ageing and was in poor health. In short, he was a disastrous choice for the command. Crozier, though a much more capable and experienced officer, and the possessor of a vast knowledge of magnetic observation, had nevertheless only recently returned from an expedition and was exhausted. Yet he could not turn down the offer of a command as it would have been detrimental to his career.

Once the expedition was underway, Franklin made crucial mistakes. Why did he leave no record of his intended movements at Beechey Island? Was this an oversight or did he think that, by leaving nothing, the Admiralty would assume he had followed instructions and had proceeded down Peel Sound? It would prove to be a fatal error. A simple message stating that he was heading down Peel Sound would have led to search expeditions looking in that direction sooner. He also made a dreadful blunder by allowing the two ships to travel in tandem. The purpose of sending two ships was to allow one to go to the other's aid if it sank or became beset. Franklin's inexperience of Arctic sea expeditions led to both ships becoming beset in the same place. There is also no evidence to suggest that Franklin laid in food depots along their original route, which meant the crews would not later head back overland in that direction. If they had done so they may have met one of the numerous expeditions that later searched for them in that direction.

When Crozier found himself in command in June 1847 he had very few options. He could not, for example, hope to reach the large depot of food at Fury Beach. Instead, he had to head south in the hope that his men could shoot seals, caribou, birds and suchlike to provide the food they desperately needed. But this turned out to be an extremely bad year for game, a fact confirmed by the hardships of the Inuit at that time. In sum, Crozier's men found themselves ill equipped, badly clothed and without food or the chance of finding enough animals to survive on. The result was inevitable – slow starvation and death as they marched miserably southwards. As Martyn Beardsley later wrote in his biography of Franklin:

> For what it is worth, I believe that, as on Franklin's calamitous first overland expedition, a number of factors, none of them necessarily fatal taken in isolation, combined to form a deadly recipe for disaster.[81]

One of the most contentious issues surrounding the Franklin expedition was the question of cannibalism – something debated ceaselessly since 1854. Rae believed the Inuit he met, who told him of finding evidence of cannibalism. This, however, was at odds with the Victorian public's image of Franklin as a doomed hero. It was preferable to think that these men slowly starved without recourse to what Rae described as 'the last resource'. Without rehearsing the entire debate here, it is sufficient to point out that modern analysis of bones retrieved from the bodies of expedition members have shown signs of cannibalism. Some argue that this was the work of the Inuit, and there is a continued reluctance to admit that these desperate Europeans could have resorted to eating human flesh. Indeed, Rebecca Harris, leader of the 2003 American Express Franklin Memorial Expedition, discounted the cannibalism theory in a recent interview in the *Geographical*. She stated:

> I don't believe that happened at all. I feel that these men have been given such an unfair press. I think their death is a lot simpler than people make out. They probably had scurvy and died of cold injuries.[82]

This attitude could be considered naive in the extreme, especially when one considers that Franklin's 1819–22 overland expedition had ended in starvation, murder and cannibalism. The crews of *Erebus* and *Terror* found themselves in a similarly disastrous situation, only on a much larger scale. Yet Harris' attitude illustrates not only the seriousness of the continued debate but also the Victorian public's ability to create and sustain heroic myths.

It is true to say that the Franklin myth has endured. Since the 1850s successive generations of explorers have returned to King William Island, the Adelaide Peninsula and the estuary of the Great Fish River in search of Franklin relics and records. Among them was Captain C.F. Hall, who searched the area in 1860 and again between 1864 and 1869. In many ways, Hall represented an exaggerated manifestation of the Victorian obsession with the Franklin story. He spent years living among the Inuit, searching for news of survivors. He later wrote:

> What burned within my soul like a living fire

all the time was the full faith that I should find
some survivors of Sir John's memorable expedition, living among the natives, and that I
would be the instrument in the hand of
heaven, of their salvation.[83]

During his extended stay in the Arctic, Hall travelled the
route the retreating crews had taken, erecting the occasional monument of stones and holding lonely religious
services on the beach.

Further searches were undertaken during the nineteenth century, including that of Lieutenant Frederick
Schwatka, who carried out a series of searches during
1878–80. Such expeditions continued throughout the
twentieth century.

What makes people return again and again in search
of traces of the expedition? It is surely the enormity of the
disappearance – two ships and 129 men – shackled to the
modern belief that a definitive solution can be found for
every mystery, and rumours of caches of documentary
records that have abounded since the mid-nineteenth
century. The Inuit told various explorers of having found
records. In some stories, these were piled up in a boat; in
others, they were in metal cans on Montreal Island. Some
accounts told of how a vault had been dug and filled with
ships' logs and journals, while further accounts talked
of the records being packed into a huge stone cairn.

One of the most puzzling aspects of the whole affair at
the time was the lack of any documentary evidence. Despite
the fact that it was standard practice to carry journals and
diaries, and to leave records in stone cairns, none have
been found since the *Fox* expedition. It is often argued that
the Inuit broke into cairns looking for valuables and
discarded the paper records as worthless.

There is also the outstanding matter of Franklin's grave – an early Inuit account told of a large vault-like structure being constructed for a burial. Experts have also suggested that Crozier buried many documents with Franklin in the expectation of their being recovered later.

It is almost certain that some material still survives and awaits discovery. In the 1990s the late Barry Ranford found the remains of a boat along with human remains and other relics on a small island in Erebus Bay. In 2003 John Murray, the Irish explorer, and the Canadian author, David Woodman, carried out magnetic surveys off King William Island and the Adelaide Peninsula. They had six positive soundings and believe they have located the remains of one of Franklin's ships.

The Franklin myth endures and will continue to draw people to the Arctic in search of a final answer. Indeed, the phenomenon of the Franklin search has taken on a life of its own. First begun in the 1840s, it continues to this day.

CHAPTER EIGHTEEN

Transatlantic Surveyor

Following his return from the Arctic in the *Fox*, McClintock's period of leave was to last for eight months. But it was obvious to the lords of the Admiralty that he was a man of considerable skill and resource. He had acquired navigational skills and had an expertise at surveying which lay beyond the scope of many other naval officers. For this reason, he was appointed in 1860 to command an important survey expedition. A transatlantic telegraph cable had been laid down in 1858 but had ceased to function after just twenty days' use. It had been decided to lay another cable, and McClintock was chosen to survey a possible route.

In June 1860 he took command of the *Bulldog*, a 1,124-ton paddle steamer being fitted out at Portsmouth. He modified the deck configuration of the ship, having a steam engine fitted to power the ten Brooke's sounding machines it carried. Among his officers for this expedition were Lieutenant Charles Parry – son of the famous Arctic explorer, Sir Edward Parry – and Lieutenant Henry Grey, whom McClintock had tried to have assigned to the *Fox* expedition.

The 1858 cable had been laid in a single, continuous

line across the Atlantic, which had led to poor telegraphic reception and made it impossible to repair once it had broken down. It was decided that a new cable would be laid in four lengths – none of which would exceed 500 miles – and it was proposed that these sections would run as follows: Scotland to the Faroe Islands; Faroe Islands to Iceland; Iceland to Greenland; Greenland to Labrador.

McClintock left Portsmouth and took the *Bulldog* northwards to the Faroe Islands, which he reached in late June 1860. On 11 July he put into Reykjavik before surveying the run to Cape Vallöe on Greenland, a distance of 600 miles. The seas to the west of Greenland were choked with ice, and a difficult three-week period was spent battling through gale-force winds en route to Godhaab. On 18 August McClintock left Greenland to complete the line of soundings as far as Hamilton Inlet on the coast of Labrador. On reaching Hamilton Inlet, he navigated through the Northwest River for a distance of 115 miles and put in at the Hudson's Bay Company depot.

McClintock next took the *Bulldog* from Hamilton Inlet through the Strait of Belleisle as far as Sydney on Cape Breton. The preceding period had been one of hard work, discomfort and not a little danger, and the stop at Sydney saw several of the crew desert. Undaunted, McClintock headed back towards Greenland, reaching Julianshaab on 29 September, before heading to Iceland on 3 October. The weather had been steadily disimproving, and the *Bulldog* – fitted as a paddle steamer – was not best suited to weather it. On the run to Iceland, McClintock encountered severe weather, the gales reaching hurricane force on 10 October. Boats were washed overboard and there was damage to the *Bulldog's* hull, masts and rudder. It was a badly damaged ship and a much-relieved McClintock that limped into Reykjavik on 16 October.

After making repairs, he put to sea again in the hope of making a final run to Portsmouth. The expedition was dogged with bad weather, however, and he had to put into Killybegs on the coast of Donegal for shelter. With a battered ship and a much reduced crew, McClintock arrived back in Portsmouth on 20 November 1860 to be praised by the Admiralty for his efforts.

Allen Young, in command of the *Fox*, was now directed by the Admiralty to retrace McClintock's journey in the hope of locating suitable places to run the telegraph cable ashore. All these efforts came to nothing. The reports of McClintock and Young were studied closely, and it was concluded that telegraph stations could not be maintained at such remote places, and that the actions of ice would cut through the cables. After much time, expense and risk, the project was abandoned.

In some respects, the *Bulldog* expedition marked the end of the 'unorthodox' phase of McClintock's career. From this time on, his postings would follow the normal path of a Victorian naval officer, though he still enjoyed both celebrity status and royal approval. In 1861 he was appointed to command the 32-gun frigate, *Doris*, in the Mediterranean. During 1862 he escorted the Prince of Wales – the future Edward VII – and the Crown Prince and Princess of Prussia on a tour of North Africa, Egypt and the Ionian Islands. Such royal connections could only benefit his career. He also had an opportunity to visit places such as Tripoli, Rhodes, Carthage and Jerusalem.

In November 1863 he took command of the *Aurora*, and in 1864 witnessed the first and last naval action of his life – but as an onlooker, not a participant. McClintock was dispatched with the *Aurora* to Heligoland in the company of a tender, the *Black Eagle*, with orders to observe naval actions between Denmark and the Prussian and Austrian governments over the disputed sovereignty of Schleswig-Holstein. His orders were to protect British merchant ships – a sensitive mission in that, had he had handled it badly, Britain could have been drawn into the war. On hearing that an Austrian squadron under Commodore Tegetthoff was at Cuxhaven, he went there aboard the *Black Eagle*. Dressed in civilian clothes, he made discreet enquiries – one could say that he played the spy – and on learning that action in the Baltic was imminent, he returned to the *Aurora* at Heligoland.

The next few days were extremely tense and dangerous. On 7 May 1864 the *Aurora* was sighted off Heligoland and, believing it was a Danish frigate, the Austrian squadron sailed out to engage her. On establishing the *Aurora*'s identity, the Austrian squadron returned to Cuxhaven. On the morning of 9 May the Austrians sailed out of Cuxhaven to meet the Danes, and McClintock took the *Aurora* to the 3-mile limit off Heligoland. The subsequent battle was brief and decisive. After an hour of continuous shelling, the Austrian flagship, the *Schwartzenburg*, was badly damaged and on fire. Soon afterwards, the Danish squadron manoeuvred across the sterns of the *Radetsky* and the remaining Austrian gun boats before shelling them. Commodore Tegetthoff prudently ordered his damaged ships to head into the neutral waters off Heligoland.

McClintock had watched the battle from the masthead of the *Aurora*, noting the tactics of the opposing squadrons and the performance of their ships. This was the first major naval battle involving steam-powered ships, and he sent his report of the battle back to England aboard the *Black Eagle*. He also offered Tegetthoff medical assistance, an offer that was politely declined. By 18 May McClintock had brought the *Aurora* safely home, having completed this delicate and risky mission.

In October he escorted the Prince and Princess of Wales during their visit to the Baltic, spending time with them in Denmark and Sweden. In Copenhagen he was presented at the Danish court, and later described the event in a letter to Lady Franklin:

> The Danish court is a very quiet one. The Royal Family are simple in their tastes, friendly in their manners and much attached to each other . . . I have dined several times with them at the court. Everyone speaks English fluently. The Crown Prince having shown considerable interest in my *Fox* voyage, I sent him my book which he has acknowledged in a nice little note.[84]

He continued:

> I was introduced to the Crown Prince of Russia, the future husband of the Princess Dagmar. Apart from the interest of seeing and talking to the future Emperor of Russia, I was glad to see him.[85]

Copenhagen had Arctic connections for McClintock. He went to the Ethnographical Museum, where he viewed artefacts donated by Petersen and 'an Esquimaux costume of mine' – presumably an exhibit he had donated to the museum. He also discovered that the *Fox*, now owned by the Royal Greenland Company, was still plying the waters off Greenland as a cargo ship.

In February 1865 he was posted to the West Indies station, where he was involved in putting down disturbances among the African community in Barbados. Later in the same year he was promoted to commodore and put in command of the squadron at Jamaica. During this time, he was not overworked, having a large staff to carry out the day-to-day running of the station. He busied himself in completing his monograph on sledge travel, and played a very public role in helping to combat the yellow-fever epidemic of 1867.

In 1868 – his posting at an end – McClintock returned to Ireland and enjoyed a period of leave. With no future posting immediately in the offing, he decided to try for Parliament in the general election of that year. Several of his ancestors had been Members of Parliament, and following their example, he offered himself as a candidate for the town of Drogheda. He could hardly have chosen a more turbulent period in Irish history in which to stand for Parliament, and would live to regret this decision.

Most sources state that he stood in the Conservative interest, and he is noted as a Tory candidate in B.M. Walker's *Parliamentary Election Results in Ireland*. In his pre-election notices, however, he announced himself as an independent candidate, and set out his proposals in *The Irish Times* of 17 November 1868 in an address to the 'independent electors of Drogheda':

> Gentleman – I have been invited by many influential members of your body to offer myself as a candidate for your suffrage at the approaching elections. I feel deeply impressed with the honour thus conferred upon me and I now beg to accept the invitation with the expression of my best thanks for the opportunity of attaching myself with the most influential town in my native county. In whatever part of the world it was my lot to be cast, I can truly say I never ceased to take a lively interest in every question

which from time to time arose, affecting the happiness and prosperity of my fellow countrymen. If elected I shall enter Parliament as an Independent member, declining to be amenable to any whip. Mr Gladstone proposes, not only the disendowment of the Established Church of Ireland, but also the disendowment of the College of Maynooth and the Presbyterian Church, and invites us to place at his disposal several hundreds of thousands a year now expended exclusively in Ireland. He declines to state his views as to the appropriation of this large income, representing a capital sum exceeding fifteen millions sterling. I apprehend it is Mr Gladstone's intention to withdraw that sum from Ireland for Imperial purposes, but no matter what may be the application which he contemplates, I decline to be a party to any such act of spoliation.[86]

McClintock also promised to press for the reform of the town's harbour board and of the Irish spirit trade.

Confident that his arguments would be welcomed by the electorate, he prepared for the election. Yet pleasing the electorate turned out to be the least of McClintock's problems. It is no exaggeration to state that Ireland was in political turmoil. The year preceding the election – 1867 – had been one of disturbances and agrarian outrage, and one which saw the outbreak and suppression of the Fenian Rebellion. There was still an air of simmering discontent in the country. Behind the Fenian agitations, there ran a deeper discontent with the political system; the majority of the Irish people, it must be remembered, had no vote in the elections. In 1862, for example, the population of Drogheda stood at over 17,500, yet only 587 people in the town had the vote. This situation was repeated all over the country, and the weeks leading up to the elections saw many electoral riots attributable to the fact that, for the majority of the population, the only way to effect the outcome of the election was to intimidate those who actually had the vote. Newspaper reports of the 1868 election in Ireland are one long catalogue of electoral disturbances. In Sligo town, one man was seized by a mob and shot. In Limerick, four people where killed, and the riots even spilled over into Irish communities in England, in places such as Blackburn, Wigan and Wakefield.

Some of the worst violence took place in Drogheda, where the sitting incumbent, the Liberal Member of Parliament, Benjamin Whitworth, employed 'bludgeon men' to intimidate voters. The day of the election – 21 November – witnessed the worst scenes. Voters were ferried in by train under police and army escort, and a riot broke out at the train station. Some of the troops panicked and opened fire, killing one man. The disturbances continued around the polling station, and when only 130 votes were cast, McClintock left the town with a police escort. Whitworth was declared the victor having polled 365 votes against McClintock's 138.

Having faced so much danger during his life, McClintock was not about to be intimidated by such conduct, and lodged a petition of protest, citing 'gross intimidation during the election' – one of several petitions lodged to appeal election results around the country. He was greatly assisted in his campaign by reports published in *The Irish Times*, which included a list of electors who had been assaulted. The full list, the editor claimed, would run to over 300 names. In a letter to the

London *Times* on 1 December 1868 McClintock stated:

> I affirm that the account of the rioting given
> by your correspondent is substantially correct:
> that the report of an Orange mob coming
> down from Dublin was a false report; and that
> very many of my supporters were prevented by
> force, or deterred by the well-founded appre-
> hensions of personal violence, from recording
> their vote.[87]

Successful in his petition, the result of the Drogheda election was declared void in January 1869. Showing considerable wisdom, he declined to stand in the new election
which followed. It had been an ill-judged foray into politics, and he had been naive to attempt to enter the political scene at such a turbulent time. He put it behind him
as an embarrassing and bruising affair.

Yet the outcome of the 1868 election had not been
entirely negative for McClintock. One of his supporters
was Mr Robert Foster Dunlop of Monasterboice House in
County Louth, and McClintock accepted an invitation to
stay with the Dunlops during the election petition. He
was greatly taken with Dunlop's second daughter, Annette
Elizabeth, and the couple formed an attachment. In
October 1870 they were married at the church at Melli-
font, the ceremony being conducted by his kinsman, the
Reverend Robert Le Poer McClintock.

Following his marriage, McClintock and his wife
moved to a new house at 2 (later renumbered as 12)
Eaton Terrace, in London.[88] In the course of a long and
happy marriage, Leopold and Annette had three sons and
two daughters. Their eldest son was Henry Foster
McClintock (1871–1959), a post office official who would

end his career as assistant private secretary to the post-master-general. He also served as a reserve army officer in the second Boer War and during the First World War, where he took part in the Gallipoli campaign. Their second son, John William Leopold McClintock (1874–1929), had a distinguished naval career, serving throughout the First World War. Having commanded HMS *Lord Nelson*, HMS *Dreadnought* and HMS *King George V*, he ended his career as a vice-admiral, and was awarded a CB (Companion of the Order of the Bath) and a DSO (Companion of the Distinguished Service Order). Leopold's youngest son was Robert Singleton McClintock (1876–1967), who joined the army and became a colonel of the Royal Engineers, serving in the Ashanti War, the second Boer War and the First World War. He was also awarded a DSO for wartime service. Details of the two McClintock daughters are more difficult to come by. The eldest daughter was Anna Elizabeth McClintock (1873–1939), who was to marry Sir Bernard Eyre Greenwell. The youngest daughter was Elizabeth Florence Mary McClintock (1882–1913). She never married, and died at a comparatively young age.[89]

Lady McClintock proved to be a woman of considerable resource, typical of the thousands of Irish women, of both religious traditions, who found themselves living in the far-flung corners of the British Empire – the varying circumstances of service life meant she had to move house frequently and often at short notice. Her children were born in various locations – London, Dublin and Halifax, Nova Scotia. During the course of her married life, she found herself playing host to members of the Royal Family on several occasions. She also helped in the running of fever hospitals. To her credit, she did both with equal ability. She died in May 1920.

CHAPTER NINETEEN

'Toward No Earthly Pole'

The years immediately following the election of 1868
witnessed a hectic phase in McClintock's career.
During this period, he served as naval ADC (aide-de-camp)
to Queen Victoria, was elected to the governing council
of the Royal Geographical Society in 1869 – he would
again serve in this capacity later in his career – and was
appointed admiral superintendent of Portsmouth dock-
yard in April 1872.

McClintock found time to maintain contact with his
former Arctic colleagues, especially those who, like himself, were from Ireland. When McClure died in October
1873 McClintock was shocked to learn that the Admiralty was quibbling about paying his widow a pension. He
wrote to Sophia Cracroft to enlist her help, telling her
that he and other naval officers were trying to secure Mrs
McClure a Civil List pension. In his letter, he noted that
the geographical discoveries of the Franklin Expedition
had predated those of McClure:

> Poor McClure's discovery, genuine and com-
> plete though it was, was anticipated by at least
> two and a half years. Had it been known at the

time, we should never have heard of McClure's
name at all in connection with the discovery
of the north west passage. The honour due
to the one cannot detract from that due to the
other; the claims of both are too clearly understood.[90]

Since returning from the *Fox* expedition in 1859
McClintock had stayed in contact with Lady Franklin,
corresponding with her from his various commands. She
had been awarded the Gold Medal of the Royal Geographical Society in 1860, and spent the rest of her life trying
to coax the Admiralty into erecting a memorial to her
dead husband. She also remained an important figure in
Arctic exploration, her advice and support being sought
by Sherard Osborn and George Nares prior to the Nares
expedition of 1875. By this time, her health was in decline,
and she died on 18 July 1875. She was buried in Kensal
Green Cemetery, McClintock acting as one of the pall-
bearers. Two weeks later a memorial to Sir John Franklin
was unveiled in Westminster Abbey, the inscription written
by Franklin's nephew, Alfred, Lord Tennyson. It read:

Not here! the white North has thy bones;
and thou,
Heroic sailor-soul,
Art passing on thine happier voyage now
Toward no earthly pole.

A smaller plaque, placed underneath, bore a touching
epitaph:

This monument was erected by Jane, his
widow, who, after long waiting, and sending in

search of him, herself departed, to seek to find
him in the realms of light, July 18, 1875, aged
83 years.

The capable and ever-cheerful Kellett had predeceased
Lady Franklin in March 1875. In the space of just a few
years, McClintock attended the funerals of two of his
fellow explorers and that of the great patroness of nineteenth-century polar exploration. A number of other polar
explorers had also died by this time: Sir Edward William
Parry, the commander of so many important Arctic expeditions, had died in 1855, Sir John Ross died in 1856,
and McClintock's old mentor, Sir James Clark Ross, died
in 1861. McClintock was now the most important surviving authority on polar travel.

When the Nares expedition of 1875–76 was being
planned, McClintock was asked to oversee preparations.
The expedition was led by Captain George Nares, who
had served previously in the Arctic aboard the *Resolute*.
The expedition's primary objective was to reach the
geographical North Pole. McClintock was given full
responsibility for equipping the expedition, and chose
the *Alert*, a screw-propelled ship of 751 tons. He later
bought a second ship, a Clyde-built sealer of 1,247 tons,
originally named *Bloodhound* but renamed *Discovery*.
Nares took charge of *Alert*, while *Discovery* was put under
the command of Captain Henry Stephenson.

Throughout the spring and early summer of 1875
McClintock supervised the loading of equipment and
stores. He also briefed the crews on his sledging methods
and on the importance of establishing supply depots.
Although the expedition would eventually acquire sledge-
dogs on Greenland, most of the sledge travel would
depend on man-hauling.

At the end of May 1875 the Nares expedition left Portsmouth. It was a gruelling time, and many of the men became ill. Nares failed to reach the North Pole, and his expedition returned to England in November 1876. Though many viewed the expedition as a complete failure, McClintock was supportive of Nares and his men, pointing out that they had surveyed over 300 miles of new coastline.

During 1876 McClintock witnessed the return of the troops from the Ashanti War, a punitive military expedition led by Dublin-born General Sir Garnet Wolseley. McClintock noticed that the troops suffered from the cold on disembarking at Portsmouth, having spent the previous months in a warm African climate. He had an awning built on the quayside, and provided the disembarking troops with hot food and drinks. Shortly after, he founded the Transport Guild, a charitable movement whose members raised funds to purchase warm clothes and other comforts for troops returning from warmer climates. For the remainder of his life, McClintock would play a prominent role in various philanthropic organisations, including the Royal Naval Scripture Readers' Society and the Royal Alfred Aged Merchant Seaman's Institute.

McClintock was promoted to vice-admiral in August 1877, and in November 1879 was appointed commander-in-chief of the North American and West Indian station, with his headquarters at Bermuda. While Bermuda was considered to be a pleasant posting, McClintock had to remain sensitive to the possibility of a clash between the French and British fishing fleets in the waters off Newfoundland.

He still enjoyed a level of royal patronage, and acted as host to both the Prince of Wales and the Duke of

Clarence during their visit to Bermuda in 1880. During a visit to Quebec, he was the guest of honour at a formal dinner hosted by Lord Lorne, the governor-general of Canada.

Using HMS *Northampton* as his flag ship, McClintock enjoyed a successful tour of duty at Bermuda, and played a prominent role in preparing a number of young officers for their later careers. His flag officer was Captain – later Admiral – Sir John A. Fisher, who was to play a major role in modernising the Royal Navy in the years prior to the First World War, and who would create a political storm when resigning as first sea lord in an act of protest over the botched Gallipoli landings.

McClintock remained interested in Arctic expeditions, and read the accounts of Hall and Schwatka's travels, commenting on them in later editions of the *Voyage of the* Fox.

Whenever he visited Ireland, he stayed with his brother, Dr Alfred Henry McClintock (1821–1881). During the course of a long medical career, Alfred had introduced much-needed sanitary reforms to Dublin's maternity wards, and was elected president of the Royal College of Surgeons in Ireland in 1880. He published widely on medical topics, and was renowned as a lecturer and philanthropist. Over the course of several visits and periods of leave, Leopold stayed with him at a succession of addresses in Dublin – Rutland Square, Hardwicke Street and 21 Merrion Square North. When his younger brother's health became a source of great worry to Leopold – in 1880 – he took him on a cruise off the coast of America and the West Indies. Alfred's health continued to decline, and Leopold was devastated when he died in October 1881.[91]

On completing his tour of duty on the American station, McClintock returned to England in January 1883,

21 Merrion Square North, Dublin – home of Dr Alfred Henry McClintock. Leopold spent periods of leave living at this address.

and was due for compulsory retirement the following year on age grounds. The voluntary retirement of a senior admiral allowed McClintock to take a final step up the *Navy List*, and he retired as a full admiral in 1884.

The years of his retirement were to be active ones. He remained involved with both the Royal Geographical Society – serving as vice-president – and the United Services Institution, and became a committee member of the National Lifeboat Institution (now the Royal National Lifeboat Institution). Despite the humiliation he had faced in the 1868 election, he remained interested in Irish politics, and became a prominent member of the Primrose League and other Conservative clubs. 1886 saw the introduction of Gladstone's first Home Rule bill, a measure McClintock vocally opposed. He would become a prime mover in unionist opposition to Home Rule, regularly having letters published in the pages of *The Times*.

He had been elected as an Elder Brother of Trinity House in 1884, and after his retirement threw himself into his duties as a commissioner of lighthouses and light-ships. Despite the fact that he was getting on in years, he regularly went on cruises of inspection, visiting Denmark and the Shetland Islands on Trinity House business. He also played a prominent role in several commissions on maritime signalling.

In 1887 McClintock was awarded a good service pension. In 1891 he was created a KCB (Knight Commander of the Order of the Bath). As he grew older, and as the numbers of Arctic veterans dwindled, he came to be regarded as the 'Grand Old Man' of polar exploration. In 1891 he helped organise the Arctic section of the Naval Exhibition at Greenwich, lending many exhibits from his own collection. When, in May 1895, a formal dinner was held at Greenwich commemorating the fiftieth anniversary of the Franklin expedition, McClintock was the guest of honour. In his after-dinner speech, he commented on the fate of the expedition:

> In laying down their lives at the call of duty our countrymen bequeathed to us a rich gift – another of those noble examples not yet rare in our history, and of which we are all so justly proud, one more beacon of light to guide our sons to deeds of heroism in the future. These examples of unflinching courage, devotion to duty, and endurance of hardships are as life-blood to naval enterprise.[92]

These were interesting comments. McClintock was apparently fully convinced of the heroism of Franklin and his men, despite the fact that there was no real evidence that any of them had been heroic. In the depths of their suffering and privation, they must have explored the darkest regions of human despair. Yet the history of the expedition was a catalogue of failures – in planning and leadership. In this instance, McClintock was advocating the notion of the 'heroic failure', and the nineteenth century was indeed full of such failures. The story of the demise of Franklin and his men could be woven into a rich quilt of Victorian failures, which included the Charge of the Light Brigade, the loss of the *Birkenhead* and General Gordon's death at Khartoum. During the next fifteen years or so, other failures would be raised to the status of mythical events, the epitome being the deaths of Captain Scott and his party in the Antarctic.

At the end of his career, McClintock found himself acting as mentor to a new generation of explorers. When

Scott was making his preparation for the British National Antarctic Expedition of 1901–04, he approached McClintock for advice on sledge travelling, equipment and rations. McClintock was appointed to the expedition's ship committee and, with Sir Clements Markham, instructed the naval architects W.E. Smyth and Son as to the required specifications for the ship. McClintock had been very pleased with the performance of the Clyde-built *Discovery* during the Nares expedition, and he recommended that Scott's ship be built along the same lines. Also named *Discovery*, it remains the most famous expedition ship to have sailed the polar regions.

McClintock's input into the preparations for Scott's expedition marked the end of his career in a practical sense. While he remained involved in the work of Trinity House, his health went into decline and, in his last years, he suffered a series of illnesses. During his years of Arctic service, he had been affected by regular bouts of snow-blindness, and his eyes had been permanently damaged. Despite a series of operations for cataracts, the strength of character and body that had typified him in his youth gave him the resilience to carry on.

In 1907, with the fiftieth anniversary of the *Fox* expedition approaching, McClintock organised a commemorative luncheon. Held on the anniversary of the sailing of the *Fox*, the guests included George Taubman Goldie, president of the Royal Geographical Society, and Sir Allen Young, who had served as navigating officer on the *Fox*. In a letter of thanks, Goldie, Young and Clements Markham wrote:

> The discoverer of the fate of the Franklin Expedition bears a name that will never be forgotten by his countrymen. Your book has long

been, and will continue to be, one of the classic narratives of our language, recording a great achievement simply and modestly, yet in a way which fills the reader with sympathy and interest. It is not for us to refer to your long and valuable subsequent services in the Navy and at Trinity House; but we may express our deep sense of the value of what you have continued to do in the interests of geography and discovery during a long course of years. You have lived to see much valuable and some splendid work achieved in the Arctic regions, but no one has approached your unequalled journeys, and you still continue to be the greatest, as you are the first of Arctic sledge travellers.[93]

In the event, McClintock did not long outlive the anniversary of that most famous expedition. During the rest of that summer, he suffered further bouts of ill health. In early autumn, he failed to shake off a cold, which developed into pneumonia. Despite the best efforts of his doctors, he died on 17 November 1907.

His funeral to Kensington Cemetery, Hanwell was massively attended. Edward VII was represented, while George Taubman Goldie led a large contingent from the Royal Geographical Society. There was an equally large contingent from Trinity House. The naval officers were led by the first sea lord, Admiral Sir John Fisher. The Royal Greenland Company, which by now owned the *Fox*, sent a memorial – a model of the ship cast in silver. Scattered among the mourners were old sailors who had served with him during his later commands, interspersed with a handful of Arctic veterans. The committees of the

Royal Geographical Society and the Royal Society, together with the corporation of Trinity House, later unveiled a memorial to McClintock in Westminster Abbey. Placed beneath the Franklin memorial, its inscription – accurate and to the point – was very much in keeping with McClintock's own character: 'Here also is commemorated Admiral Sir Leopold McClintock, 1819–1907. Discoverer of the Fate of Franklin in 1859'.[94]

Admiral Sir Francis Leopold McClintock was dead. Within a few short years, he would be virtually forgotten, his career remembered only by other naval men, explorers and geographers, aware as they were of the vastness of his achievements.

Francis Leopold McClintock.

CHAPTER TWENTY

Forgotten Hero

By the end of his career, Sir Francis Leopold McClintock had established himself as one of the greatest polar explorers of the nineteenth century, and had secured a place in the pantheon of Victorian heroes. For the Victorian public, McClintock was a figure of immense importance because of his discovery of the fate of Franklin and his men.

At the time of his retirement, he had accumulated more time at sea than any other officer in the Royal Navy. The 'Arctic Fox' had begun his career as a polar explorer when this form of exploration was still in its infancy, and had survived to advise a new generation of explorers as they commenced the next phase of polar exploration – men such as Scott and Shackleton. In his 50-odd years in the navy, McClintock had witnessed vast changes in technology and naval practice. A witness to the navy's transition from sail to steam, he had been one of the first generation of officers to be trained in the use of steam-powered engines.

McClintock was a pioneer and a hero. Yet even in his own lifetime there were voices of dissent. Some pointed out that the evidence collected by Dr John Rae predated

McClintock's discoveries. William Arrowsmith, the noted cartographer, championed Rae's prior claims, and this sparked a lively correspondence between the two explorers. In March 1860 Rae opened what was to become a lengthy debate. In a letter to McClintock he stated:

> It is very generally allowed that the information brought home by me in 1854, together with the numerous relics bearing the crests and initials of fourteen of the officers of the *Erebus* and *Terror*, were sufficient evidence that a large portion of both Franklin's ships had died of disease and starvation in the neighbourhood of the Back River and King William's Land on, or previous to, 1850 and that these were the last survivors of the party. I was also told that the ship or ships had been destroyed by ice. Your information does not contradict that brought by me in any important fact, and proves the correctness of the Esquimaux intelligence even in regard to the route followed by the unfortunate people on their way to the Back River. You leave 102 persons out of 129 unaccounted for, except through information similar to that from which mine was obtained – *my* interpreter was perfectly acquainted with the dialogue and language of the Esquimaux of Repulse Bay, many of whom I had known in 1846–7, and had always found, with few exceptions, honest and truthful. There are other more minute particulars that I might dwell upon, but the great fact that a large portion of Franklin's party died of starvation and (leaving little doubt as to the fate of the

remainder) at a certain locality which I named correctly on, or before, 1850, was communicated by me in 1854.[95]

McClintock replied by letter, written in Dublin:

> I quite agree with *all* you state as to the information and relics brought home by you in '54; they afforded circumstantial evidence as to the fate of a large party, probably the last survivors of Franklin's crews; and the impression was strong as to the sad fate of the whole. But positive proof was wanting, therefore in '55 Anderson was sent out by the government but he was unable to do more than confirm your locality of Montreal Island. In '59 I confirmed more of your report and found such further traces and records as have cleared up the fate of the whole expedition. Now it is evident that these traces were unknown to the natives themselves, no information respecting them could have reached you; therefore these skeletons, records, several cairns and a boat, besides articles innumerable are my discovery. Also, by having been able to judge of their equipment from specimens seen, of their state of health, and of the absence of game upon the coast they travelled, I have shown that they could not possibly have reached beyond Montreal Island and must have all perished. This should not be confused with the information you received respecting those who died upon the mainland. All native information whether obtained by you or I must be limited to the SW shore of King

William Island, since they have not visited the NW coast. But you will see that I have managed my work as to be independent of their testimony altogether. My object in the *Fox* was to examine the whole of the unexplored area between the Barrow Strait beaches and Anderson and I did so. Had your information as to locality been conclusive this great labour would have been unnecessary. Now in spite of these additional and important facts, Arrowsmith does me the injustice of giving you credit for the *whole*, and simply mentioned me as having 'fully confirmed' you, and talks of 'the first intelligence of the Fate' as if anything could be *discovered twice*.[96]

It is obvious from the tone of McClintock's letter that he considered the matter closed. He was far from correct in this assumption, and an irritable correspondence continued between the two explorers for years. Indeed, the debate continues to this day, with many experts on polar history championing Rae's prior claims to having discovered the ultimate fate of the Franklin expedition. Others continue to point out that McClintock found actual evidence, and that his expedition also discovered the only documentary record left by Franklin's men. The debate is sure to continue, but it may be more worthwhile to simply accept that *both* men played their part in solving the Franklin mystery.

A tragic fact often overlooked by later polar historians was that, during his first expedition to the Arctic with Sir James Clark Ross in 1848–49, McClintock had come quite close to solving the Franklin mystery. Having explored North Somerset and travelling southwards to within 50 miles of Cape Bird, Ross and McClintock came close to discovering evidence of Franklin's men. Ross was later criticised for revisiting the area of his magnetic North Pole expedition. Yet in 1859 McClintock would meet Inuit near the magnetic North Pole who told him of the fate of the Franklin expedition. McClintock's first expedition, therefore, came within a hair's breadth of discovering evidence of the missing men. What made this doubly tragic was that the Inuit told of hearing the gunfire of hunting parties from the *Erebus* and *Terror* as late as May 1850. The expedition of Ross and McClintock in 1848–49 probably represented the only real chance of rescue that the survivors of the Franklin expedition ever had.

McClintock's geographical contributions were of major significance. During the course of successive voyages, he surveyed hundreds of miles of coastline and his discoveries redrew the map of the Arctic. He mapped the coastlines of North Somerset, Melville Island, Prince Patrick Island and King William Island, while also discovering the Polnia Islands and a navigable Northwest Passage. The 'blank spaces' on Admiralty charts that had so bothered Sir John Barrow had been largely filled in by the end of McClintock's career, though Barrow himself did not live to see it.

As McClintock discovered and surveyed these new lands, he also named them, and many Arctic place names owe their origins to his survey expeditions. McClintock chose numerous place names to honour the men of the missing expedition – such as the Franklin Channel – while also naming places after the crew of the *Fox*. There are places in the Arctic named after McClintock himself, applied by Ross and Austin: McClintock Cape on Prince Patrick Island, McClintock Point on North Somerset and the McClintock Channel, which flows between Prince of

Wales Island and Victoria Island. When raising funds for the *Fox* expedition, he promised subscribers he would name some newly discovered place in the Arctic in their honour. Sir Thomas Dyke Acland subscribed £100, for which McClintock named Acland Bay in his honour. Sir Charles Nicholson subscribed just £3, and despite the paltry nature of the donation, Nicholson Cape was named after him. The writer, W.M. Thackeray, donated £5, and had Thackeray Point named in his honour. This tactic of naming places after subscribers was useful for raising funds, and Sir Ernest Shackleton would later employ similar methods in his fund-raising efforts.

Being typically Victorian, McClintock was an avid collector. Throughout his expeditions, he collected geological and zoological specimens. Though possessed of great curiosity, he lacked the scientific knowledge to grasp the full significance of his collection, and it was later shown to contain material of great scientific importance. In 1860 he deposited a collection of over 370 fossils in the museum of the Royal Dublin Society – eleven of these represented species then unknown to science. At a meeting of the Dublin University Zoological and Botanical Association, McClintock was presented with an illuminated address. The president of the association, Dr Samuel Haughton, said in his speech:

> Whether we estimate the additions made to the sciences of zoology and geology by our distinguished member, by the value of the presents he has made to the Royal Dublin Society, or whether we consider the important inferences that can be drawn from them, it is impossible to value too highly, the gift the society has received.[97]

Both Haughton and Dr Walker – the surgeon aboard the *Fox* – would later write on the importance of this collection in the *Journal of the Royal Dublin Society*. These fossils – together with stuffed specimens of a polar bear and a musk ox donated by McClintock – remain in the collection of the Natural History Museum in Merrion Row in Dublin, just a short walk away from Merrion Square where McClintock lived with his brother, Alfred.

A fascinating aspect of McClintock's fossil hunting arises from his casual mention of being unable to carry all his specimens back from his expeditions. He later remarked that some of this material had been abandoned or cached. One such cache was discovered on Melville Island in 1960 by Dr Thorsteinson and Dr Tozer of the Canadian Geological Survey, who found a cache of fossils under a cairn, many of which still bore McClintock's own labels. The Dublin fossil collection was subsequently taken to Canada to enable a comparative study.

McClintock did not confine his collection to fossil hunting. In his interactions with the Inuit, he traded with them for samples of their material culture. A small collection of this material – including a stone lamp, a bone knife, a hunting lance, and a kayak and paddle – was later donated by McClintock to the Royal Dublin Society. The collection is now held in the National Museum of Ireland, located at Collins Barracks, Dublin. Though only a small collection, these early Inuit pieces acquired by McClintock display no European influences, and represent an important 'first contact' collection.[98]

It is not commonly known that McClintock was also one of the first to practice photography in the polar regions. In light of great public excitement at the work of early photographers – such as Fox Talbot and Roger Fenton – many Arctic expeditions of this period carried

Natural History Museum, Dublin, repository for several of
McClintock's specimens, including his polar bear and musk ox.

primitive photographic equipment. Indeed, the Franklin expedition carried a daguerreotype apparatus, and during his searches, McClintock hoped to find photographic plates from the expedition. The disastrous Belcher expedition of 1852–54 had a calotype apparatus among its equipment, and this was initially entrusted to the care of Dr William Domville, the surgeon aboard *Resolute*. Following Belcher's order to abandon *Intrepid*, McClintock found himself with spare time, and experimented with this calotype apparatus. His journal entry of August 1854 noted: 'I am practising with a calotype but am not very successful.' Over time, he became more proficient. In his journal entry of 8 August 1854 McClintock states that he had 'made considerable progress on the use of the calotype'. He later wrote of taking images of Beechey Island and portraits of the expedition's crew. In his journal of 21 August he wrote: 'Succeeded tolerably well with some calotype portraits', a statement supported by the journal entry of George Ford, carpenter of the *Investigator*, who noted: 'Capn McClintock after dinner taking likenesses on deck with a calotype'.

It is unfortunate that none of these portraits appear to have survived, but perhaps they are awaiting discovery in some private collection. The recent discovery in Canada of a batch of McClintock/Lady Franklin letters gives one hope. Two of McClintock's calotypes of Beechey Island survive in a private collection – one a particularly fine depiction of the *North Star* moored in Erebus and Terror Bay.

McClintock ensured that the *Fox* expedition carried photographic equipment. Dr Walker was appointed as the expedition's official photographer, and one of his images of the *Fox* beset in Baffin Bay has survived. McClintock was one of the first explorers to recognise the potential of photography and, aside from his own humble photographic attempts, encouraged others to experiment in the use of photographic equipment. In this way, he played a small but important part in the history of Arctic photography.[99]

McClintock is perhaps best remembered for his epic sledge expeditions, and is often referred to as the 'father of modern sledging technique'. When one considers that previous Arctic explorers had confined themselves to surveying coastal areas, his use of long-range sledge expeditions was of major importance. He constantly experimented with new equipment, and advocated the use of sails and kites to help reduce the burden of the sledging parties. During the course of several sledge expeditions, he perfected techniques, equipment and rations, making it possible to travel overland for many weeks, thus covering hundreds of miles in a single journey. McClintock's depot system was essential in increasing the distance a sledge party could travel, and in ensuring survival. During the course of his four Arctic voyages, McClintock's sledging experiments led to a revolution in the methods of polar travel, and his innovations would be utilised by later polar explorers. As the twentieth century got underway, Scott and Shackleton would read his writings on polar travel, and go to the man himself for advice.

Yet McClintock was very conservative in some of his attitudes to Arctic survival. While he studied and adopted Inuit hunting methods, he never properly appreciated their considerable survival skills or, for that matter, their methods of travel in the Arctic. While he experimented with the use of sledge-dogs, and wrote of their effectiveness, he still preferred to use manpower to pull sledges. This trend would characterise later British polar explorations, with twentieth-century explorers such as Scott and Shackleton both utilising manpower in preference to dog-teams. McClintock's insistence on the use of man-hauled sledges meant he could never operate in the Arctic as efficiently as the Inuit. Even in his own lifetime, other explorers – among them George Lyon and Dr John Rae – opted to live among the Inuit in order to learn their ways, and were thus able to travel and survive in the most severe conditions. In their later writings on the subject, both Lyon and Rae pointed out that the Inuit survived in conditions that routinely killed Europeans. Yet McClintock would never fully embrace Inuit ways, and his rejection of their survival methods and their use of dog-teams meant that later British explorers who turned to him for advice would be infected with this prejudice.

Roald Amundsen, the great Norwegian explorer, was influenced by McClintock's writings while still only a child. Amundsen read accounts of the expeditions of McClintock, McClure, Collinson and Rae, and was determined to find a navigable Northwest Passage. Having spent time living with the Inuit, Amundsen succeeded in his goal with the *Gjøa* expedition of 1903–06, concluding in the process that it was too difficult a passage to be a practical trade route. The methods Amundsen learned from the Inuit regarding polar survival and the use of dog-teams enabled him to lead a successful expedition to the South Pole in 1911, while Scott – still relying on man-hauling – would perish with his team in the Antarctic wastes, thus graphically illustrating the shortcomings of McClintock's ideas regarding polar survival. Indeed, in his own lifetime he had acknowledged that his methods were extremely hard on his men, describing man-hauling as the 'most excessive' labour.

Despite the renown McClintock achieved in his own lifetime and the impact he made in the fields of exploration and scientific discovery, he is largely unknown today. The recent resurgence in interest in polar history has focused on Scott, Nansen, Amundsen and Shackleton; though all were influenced in some way by McClintock's experiences and writings, he remains largely forgotten, and is often only briefly referred to in exploration histories. Nor was he the subject of any large public memorials. There are few physical reminders of McClintock. A small plaque on the house where he was born, and the specimens he donated to various museums, are the most obvious relics of his life. Stephen Pearce, the portraitist, painted three portraits, now held in the National Portrait Gallery in London. The sculptor, Joseph Robinson Kirk, carved a bust of McClintock, now to be found in the collection of the Royal Dublin Society. Another bust – carved by McClintock's daughter, Anna – is displayed in St Ann's Church in Portsmouth.

The reputation of Francis Leopold McClintock continues to be admired by a small population of polar historians and enthusiasts, and people in the most far-flung places do still remember him. Stephen Reynolds, manager of the Canadian side of the Yukon Quest – renowned as the toughest sledge-dog race in the world – has informed me that many dog-sledgers still regard McClintock as one of the greatest Arctic travellers. Indeed, a township in the Yukon is named after McClintock. Perhaps he would have wanted it this way – to be remembered among the men and women who continue to travel in Arctic conditions, and who use methods that have remained largely unchanged since his own day.

1 Mary Shelley, *Frankenstein* (1818 edn.). In the same year, Captain John Ross, Lieutenant Edward Parry, Captain David Buchan and Lieutenant John Franklin took the ships *Isabella*, *Alexander*, *Trent* and *Dorothea* to the Arctic in search of a Northwest Passage.

2 Sarah L. Steele, *The Right Honourable Arthur MacMorrough Kavanagh* (1891); see also Donald McCormick, *The Incredible Mr Kavanagh* (London, 1960).

3 *Burke's Irish Family Records* (1976), pp. 750–5.

4 Ibid. See also *Dictionary of National Biography* and Sir Clements Markham, *Life of Sir Leopold McClintock* (London, 1909).

5 *Navy List*, 1832.

6 Astley Cooper Key, *The Recovery of HMS* Gorgon (London, 1847).

7 Markham, op. cit, p. 30.

8 The best modern account of the search for the Northwest Passage is probably Ann Savours', *The Search for the North West Passage* (London, 1999).

9 Fergus Fleming, *Barrow's Boys* (London, 1998).

10 J.H. Tuckey, *Narrative of an Expedition to Explore the River Zaire* (London, 1818). This account was published posthumously.

11 As late as 1849, William R. O'Byrne's *A Naval Biographical Dictionary* (3 vols., London, 1849) reported that Franklin was 'engaged, since 3 March 1845, in a fresh attempt to explore a north west passage through Lancaster Sound and Bering Strait'.

12 Born in 1806, Henry Kellett was the son of John Dalton Kellett; his cousin was Commander Arthur Kellett RN. Henry entered the Royal Navy in January 1822. In February 1845, he took command of the survey ship *Herald*, and carried out a survey of the coasts of Central America, the Gulf of California and Vancouver Island. Kellett travelled to the Norton and Kotzebue Sounds in Alaska in 1848 and, in July 1849, sailed again to Kotzebue Sound, and took *Herald* northwards until she was stopped by ice at 71° 12' north. North of Siberia, he discovered an island now called Kellett Island, and named another island Herald Island.

13 SPRI (Scott Polar Research Institute), McClintock's *Enterprise* Journal, 22 June 1848.

14 Ibid.

15 Ibid. 30 November 1848.

16 Ibid. 11 November 1848.

17 Ibid.

18 Captain F.L. McClintock, 'Reminiscences of Arctic Ice-Travel in Search of Sir John Franklin and His Companions', *Journal of the Royal Dublin Society*, vol. i (1858), p. 183.

19 Ibid. pp. 183–4.
20 Ibid. p. 185.
21 Ibid. p. 188.
22 Ibid. p. 192.
23 Ibid.
24 Quoted in Captain Robert F. Scott, *Voyage of the* Discovery (London, 1905) p. 300.
25 SPRI, McClintock's *Enterprise* Journal. The 'Combes' mentioned was Thomas Coombes of the *Investigator*, who died on 27 October 1848.
26 McClintock, 'Reminiscences', p. 184.
27 Ibid. p. 195.
28 During the course of the next three years, McClure would obsessively pursue the much sought-after Northwest Passage.
29 During the Famine in Ireland, Ommanney had carried out important relief work.
30 Markham, op. cit. p. 87.
31 McClintock, 'Reminiscences', p. 196.
32 Ibid. pp. 196–7.
33 McClintock, 'Reminiscences', p. 203.
34 Ibid. p. 198.
35 Markham, op. cit.
36 McClintock, 'Reminiscences', pp. 206–7.
37 Ibid. p. 199.
38 Ibid. p. 203.
39 Ibid. p. 205.
40 Ibid. pp. 207–8.
41 Colonel Neville W. Poulsom and Rear Admiral J.A.L. Myres, *British Polar Exploration and Research: a Historical and Medallic Record with Biographies, 1818–1999* (London, 2000), pp. 240–1.
42 McClintock, 'Reminiscences', p. 215.
43 Ibid. p. 216.
44 Ibid. pp. 216–7.
45 Markham, op. cit.
46 McClintock, 'Reminiscences', pp. 219–20.
47 Ibid. p. 223.
48 Ibid. p. 224.
49 Ibid. pp. 230–1.
50 Ibid. p. 232.
51 Ibid. pp. 234–5.
52 Poulsom and Myres, op. cit. Mecham had also found trees, with bark, on the west coasts of Prince Patrick Island. This piece of information fed into McClure's account of a current that flowed from west to east, and which deposited large quantities of pack ice along the coasts of Banks Island. During the winter months that followed, McClintock's mind would occasionally return to the question of this easterly flowing current. It was a major discovery, but explorers of the period – McClintock included – failed to grasp its significance. It was the Norwegian explorer, Fridtjof Nansen, who would work out its significance, and he

would utilise this current during the *Fram* expedition of 1894–96.

53 McClintock, 'Reminiscences', p. 238.

54 Ultimately, McClintock and Kellett would be proved to have been correct in their predictions about the eventual break up of the ice. Belcher was subjected to even further embarrassment when one of the ships – Kellett's *Resolute* – was salvaged in Davis Strait by Captain James Buddington aboard the American whaler, the *George Henry*. The *Resolute* was bought by the American government, refitted and presented to Queen Victoria in December 1856 as an act of goodwill. The story of the *Resolute* had a succession of curious epilogues. When she was broken up in 1880, a writing desk was made from her timbers and was sent to America to be presented to President Rutherford B. Hayes. It was later reported that President John F. Kennedy found the desk in a White House cellar, and had it brought up for his own use. Harold Wilson, when prime minister of Britain, presented President Lyndon Johnson with *Resolute*'s bell; Ann Savours, op. cit. pp. 267–9.

55 SPRI MS 248/439/9–21, McClintock to Sophia Cracroft, 28 February 1857.

56 SPRI MS 248/439/22–36, McClintock to Lady Franklin, 6 April 1857.

57 McClintock, 'Reminiscences', p. 238.

58 SPRI MS 248/439/22–36, McClintock to Lady Franklin, 18 April 1857.

59 Ibid.

60 Who was this 'Chief quartermaster'? McClintock recorded taking on William Harvey to fill this position. Harvey had served aboard the *Resolute* (1850–51) and *North Star* (1852–54). From the available records, it would appear that Harvey took part in the entire *Fox* expedition. This seems to suggest that a different quartermaster had been sent home at the start of the expedition – one whose name has not been recorded.

61 SPRI MS 248/439/38, McClintock to Lady Franklin, 28 April 1858.

62 SPRI MS 248/439/22–36, McClintock to Lady Franklin, 6 May 1858.

63 SPRI MS 248/439/22–36, McClintock to Lady Franklin, 3 June 1858.

64 SPRI MS 248/439/22–36, McClintock to Lady Franklin, 3 August 1858.

65 Sir F.L. McClintock, *The Voyage of the* Fox *in the Arctic Seas in Search of Franklin and His Companions* (6th edn., London, 1895), p. 244.

66 Ibid. p. 246.

67 Markham, op. cit. p. 225.

68 McClintock, *Voyage*, p. 249.

69 Ibid. p. 251.

70 Ibid. pp. 251–2.

71 Ibid. p. 254.

72 Ibid. p. 285.

73 SPRI MS 248/439/1–3, McClintock to the Admiralty, September 1859.

74 SPRI MS 248/439/22–36, McClintock to Lady Franklin, 21 September 1859.

75 Ibid.

76 SPRI MS 248/439/1–3, McClintock to the Admiralty, 21 September 1859.

77 G.D. Burtchaell and T.U. Sadleir, *Alumni Dublinenses* (2nd edn., Dublin, 1935).

78 *Dundalk Democrat*, 5 August 1967, quoted in Frank Nugent, *Seek the Frozen Lands* (The Collins Press, 2003), p. 138.

79 Markham, op. cit. p. 237.

80 SPRI MS 248/439/22–36, McClintock to Lady Franklin, 22 January 1860. The lord lieutenant of Ireland at this time was Lord Carlisle.

81 Martyn Beardsley, *Deadly Winter: the life of Sir John Franklin* (London, 2002), p. 234.

82 Christian Amodeo, 'Harris of the Arctic', *Geographical*, September 2003, p. 51.

83 Savours, op. cit. p. 301.

84 SPRI MS 248/439/22–36, McClintock to Lady Franklin, 19 October 1864.

85 Ibid.

86 *The Irish Times*, 17 November 1868.

87 *The Times*, 1 December 1868.

88 The McClintocks later lived at different addresses in London: 29 Kensington Gate, 8 Atherstone Terrace and 16 Queensberry Place.

89 Burke, *Irish Family Records* (1976), pp. 752–3; see also Markham, op. cit. p. 293.

90 SPRI MS 248/439/9–21, McClintock to Sophia Cracroft, 23 October 1873.

91 Information kindly provided by Ms Helen Andrews of the Royal Irish Academy's *Dictionary of Irish Biography*.

92 Quoted in Markham, op. cit. p. 291.

93 Ibid. p. 295.

94 *The Times*, 18 November 1907, 23 November 1907.

95 Ken McGoogan, *Fatal Passage: the untold story of John Rae, the Arctic adventurer who discovered the fate of Franklin* (2002), p. 147.

96 Ibid. pp. 248–9.

97 *Proceedings of the Dublin University Zoological and Botanical Association*, ii (1860), p. 34.

98 Information kindly provided by Ms Rachel Hand, ethnographical officer of the National Museum of Ireland.

99 Douglas Wamsley and William Barr, 'Early Photographers in the Arctic', *Polar Record*, vol. 32, no. 183 (October 1996), pp. 295–316.

Books and Articles

Armstrong, Alexander, *A Personal Narrative of the Discovery of the North West Passage* (London, 1857).

Barr, William (ed.), *Searching for Franklin: the land Arctic searching expedition, 1855* (Hakluyt Society, London, 1999).

Barrow, John, *Voyages of Discovery and Research within the Arctic Regions* (London, 1846).

Beardsley, Martyn, *Deadly Winter: the life of Sir John Franklin* (London, 2002).

Beattie, Owen and John Geiger, *Frozen in Time: the fate of the Franklin expedition* (London, 1987).

Berton, Pierre, *The Arctic Grail: the quest for the North West Passage and the North Pole, 1818–1909* (New York, 1988).

Boase, Frederic, *Modern English Biography* (London, 1892–1901).

Boylan, Henry, *A Dictionary of Irish Biography* (Dublin, 1998).

Browne, W.H., *Ten Coloured Views Taken during the Arctic Expedition of Her Majesty's Ships* Enterprise *and* Investigator, *under the Command of Sir James C. Ross* (London, 1850).

Burke's Landed Gentry of Ireland (London, 1912).

Burke's Irish Family Records (London, 1976).

Burtchaell, G.D. and T.U. Sadleir, *Alumni Dublinenses* (2nd edn., Dublin, 1935).

Cooper Key, Astley, *The Recovery of HMS* Gorgon (London, 1847).

Cryriax, Richard J., *Sir John Franklin's Last Arctic Expedition* (London, 1939).

D'Alton, J. and J. R. Flanagan, *History of Dundalk and its environs* (Dundalk, 1864).

Delgado, James, *Across the Top of the World: the quest for the North West Passage* (London, 1999).

Dictionary of Canadian Biography (Toronto).

Dictionary of National Biography (London).

Fiennes, Ranulph, *Captain Scott* (London, 2003).

Fleming, Fergus, *Barrow's Boys* (London, 1998).

Franklin, Sir John, *Narrative of a Journey to the Shores of the Polar Sea in the Years 1819, '20, '21 and 1822* (London, 1823).

Franklin, Sir John, *Narrative of a Second Expedition to the Shores of the Polar Sea in the Years 1825, 1826 and 1827* (London, 1828).

Holland, Clive, *Arctic Exploration and Development, c. 500 BC to 1915: an encyclopaedia* (New York and London, 1994).

Kirwan, L.P., *The White Road: a survey of polar exploration* (London, 1959).

Markham, Sir Clements, *Life of Sir Leopold McClintock* (London, 1909).

Markham, Sir Clements, *The Arctic Navy List, 1773–1873* (London, 1875).

McClintock, Captain Francis Leopold, *The Voyage of the* Fox (Konemann, 1998).

McClintock, Francis Leopold, 'Reminiscences of Arctic Ice-Travel in Search of Sir John Franklin and His Companions', *Journal of the Royal Dublin Society*, vol. i, (Dublin, 1858).

McClintock, Francis Leopold, *Voyage of the* Fox *in the Arctic Seas in Search of Franklin and His Companions* (6th edn., London, 1895).

McClure, Robert (ed. Sherard Osborn), *The Discovery of the North-West Passage by HMS* Investigator (London, 1856).

McCormick, Donald, *The Incredible Mr Kavanagh* (London, 1960).

McGoogan, Ken, *Fatal Passage: the untold story of John Rae, the Arctic adventurer who discovered the fate of Franklin* (2002).

Nanton, Paul, *Arctic Breakthrough: Franklin's expeditions, 1819–1847* (London, 1970).

Nugent, Frank, *Seek the Frozen Lands* (Cork, 2003).

O'Byrne, William R., *A Naval Biographical Dictionary* (3 vols., London, 1849).

Osborn, Sherard, *Stray Leaves from an Arctic Journal* (London, 1852).

Owen, Roderic, *The Fate of Franklin* (London, 1978).

Poulsom, Colonel Neville W. and Rear Admiral J.A.L. Myres, *British Polar Exploration and Research: a historical and medallic record with biographies, 1818–1999* (London, 2000).

Reid, Alan, *Discovery and Exploration: a concise history* (London, 1980).

Richards, Robert L., *Dr John Rae* (1994).

Savours, Ann, *The Search for the North West Passage* (London, 1999).

Scott, Captain R.F., *Voyage of the* Discovery (2 vols., London, 1905).

Seeman, Berthold, *Narrative of the Voyage of HMS* Herald *during the Years 1845–51 under the Command of Captain Henry Kellett* (2 vols., London, 1853).

Spearman, David, *Samuel Haughton: Victorian polymath* (RIA, Dublin, 2002).

Spufford, Francis, *I May Be Some Time: ice and the English imagination* (London, 1996).

Steele, Sarah L., *The Right Honourable Arthur MacMorrough Kavanagh* (1891).

Tuckey, J.H., *Narrative of an Expedition to Explore the River Zaire* (London, 1818).

Walker, Brian M., *Parliamentary Election Results in Ireland, 1801–1922* (Dublin, 1978).

Woodward, F.J., *Portrait of Jane: a life of Lady Franklin* (London, 1951).

Contemporary Directories
  Army List
  Dublin Directory
  Navy List
  Thom's Irish Almanac

Contemporary Newspapers and Journals
  Dublin Builder
  Dublin University Magazine
  London Gazette
  Proceedings of the Dublin University Zoological and Botanical
    Association
  Proceedings of the Royal Irish Academy
  Royal Dublin Society Journal
  The Illustrated London News
  The Irish Times
  The Times
  United Service Journal

Modern Newspapers and Journals
  Arctic
  Geographical Journal
  Geographical Magazine
  National Geographic
  Polar Record
  The Irish Times

Manuscripts
  Scott Polar Research Institute, Cambridge (SPRI)
    MS 1, MJ, 'Journal kept during the voyage of HMS *Enterprise*,
      May 1848 to November 1849'.
    MS 92, MJ, 'Reports of sledge journeys, 1850–51'.
    MS 216/2, MJ, 'Report to Captain Austin on sledge journey,
      October 1852'.
    MS 216/1, MJ, 'Journals of cart and sledge journeys, 1852–54'.
    MS 1, MJ, 'Journal kept during the voyage of the *Intrepid*'.
    MS 248/439/38, 'Proceedings of the *Fox*, 6 August 1857 to 28
      April 1858'.
    MS 248/439/1–3, 'Three letters from McClintock to the Admiralty'.
    MS 248/439/9–21, 'Letters from McClintock to Ms Sophia
      Cracroft'.
    MS 248/439/22–36, 'Letters from McClintock to Lady Franklin'.
    MS 1229/2, 'Letter from McClintock to Alexander Scott'.

  National Library of Ireland
    n. 424, p. 599, 'Journal of Polar expeditions, 1848–54, including
      the journal of F.L. McClintock, commander of the *Intrepid*'.

  Natural History Museum of Ireland
    McClintock file (material on zoological specimens).